T0205456

Progress in IS

More information about this series at http://www.springer.com/series/10440

Stefan Stieglitz · Christoph Lattemann
Susanne Robra-Bissantz · Rüdiger Zarnekow
Tobias Brockmann
Editors

Gamification

Using Game Elements in Serious Contexts

Springer

Editors
Stefan Stieglitz
Research Group Professional
   Communication in Electronic
   Media/Social Media, Competence Center
   Connected Organization, Department
   of Computer Science and Applied
   Cognitive Science
University Duisburg-Essen
Duisburg
Germany

Christoph Lattemann
Information Management
Jacobs University Bremen
Bremen
Germany

Susanne Robra-Bissantz
Institut für Wirtschaftsinformatik
Technische Universität Braunschweig
Braunschweig, Lower Saxony
Germany

Rüdiger Zarnekow
Information and Communication
   Management
Technical University of Berlin
Berlin
Germany

Tobias Brockmann
Innoscale AG
Berlin
Germany

ISSN 2196-8705   ISSN 2196-8713 (electronic)
Progress in IS
ISBN 978-3-319-83319-4   ISBN 978-3-319-45557-0 (eBook)
DOI 10.1007/978-3-319-45557-0

Printed on acid-free paper

This Springer imprint is published by Springer Nature
The registered company is Springer International Publishing AG
The registered company address is: Gewerbestrasse 11, 6330 Cham, Switzerland

Contents

About the Editors

Dr. Stefan Stieglitz is Professor and Head of the research group for Professional Communication in Electronic Media/Social Media at University of Duisburg-Essen, Germany. His work has been published in reputable journals including Journal of Management Information System (JMIS), Business & Information Systems Engineering (BISE), International Journal of Social Research Methodology, and Management Information Systems Quarterly Executive (MISQE). In his research, he investigates user behavior and technology adaption of information systems in organizational contexts.

Dr. Christoph Lattemann is Professor of Business Administration and Information Management at Jacobs University Bremen, Germany. His research encompasses the two major global trends: Digital Transformation and Globalization. He is the founder and director of the Design Thinking Lab at Jacobs University—the D-Forge, and director of the Jacobs Research Center for the Studies of China and Globalization.

He held Visiting Scholar positions at Harvard University, JFK School of Governance, and Stanford University. He has published 7 books and more than 150 articles. He has taught courses in top international MBA programs and universities. Previously he has held senior positions in project management in the financial industry at the German Stock Exchange and is still consulting for governmental institutions and companies.

Dr. Susanne Robra-Bissantz is Full Professor of Business Information Systems Research at Technische Universität Braunschweig, Germany, since 2007. There she holds the chair of Information Management. Her research focusses on innovative and customer-oriented e-services, with special interest in collaboration mechanisms for social media, context sensitivity, service design, and service ecosystems. She has published more than 100 peer-reviewed papers and acquired multiple projects (more than 2 Mio Euro) from industry and public funding. Before that she did her habilitation and Ph.D. at University Erlangen-Nürnberg.

Dr. Ruediger Zarnekow holds the Chair for Information and Communication Management at Technische Universitaet Berlin. His research focuses on IT management, digital business models, cloud computing, and IT service management. Previously, he worked at the Institute of Information Management at the University of St. Gallen, Switzerland, where he led the competence center "Industrialization of Information Management". Professor Zarnekow has been working as a consultant in the area of IT management and digital business models for many years. As an author he has published various books and research articles.

Dr. Tobias Brockmann studied information systems at the University of Muenster and successfully finished his Ph.D. there. He published his research on the field "Mobile Enterprise" in academic journals such as the Management of Information Systems Quarterly Executive Journal or the Mobile Information System Journal. Moreover, his work was published in international conferences such as the European Conference on Information Systems or the American Conference on Information Systems. Dr. Brockmann managed the Competence Center Connected Organization at the University of Duisburg-Essen for 2 years. Now he is co/founder and Head of Operations at innoscale AG.

List of Figures

List of Tables

Part I
Fundamentals, Concepts, and Theories of Gamification

Chapter 1
Introduction to Gamification: Foundation and Underlying Theories

Amir Matallaoui, Nicolai Hanner and Rüdiger Zarnekow

Abstract This introductory article provides basic definitions, concepts and theories surrounding gamification that are used throughout the remainder of this book. It distinguishes gamification from other research areas, such as gameful design and serious games. It then goes on to introduce common game mechanics, achievement systems, game dynamics and aesthetics. The second part of the article focusses on underlying theories. It examines the influence of motivation theory, achievement goal theory and flow theory on gamification. The article also describes different player archetypes.

1.1 Introduction

Using information systems has steadily been increasing and the penetration into everyday life and work has become increasingly important. Yet, many information systems are only used out of necessity and not because of their appeal, particularly in a working or educational context. This leads to demotivation of users, lower acceptance and unwanted behaviour and outcomes. Consequently, the question arises: how can people be motivated to change their behaviours or explore other ways of doing things? One concept that is an inextricable part of humanity is 'play' which describes doing something out of the ordinary and freely within the boundaries of time and space by following strict rules to experience the feeling of excitement and joy (Huizinga 1949). Applying this concept has led to the term gamification that is used to describe an innovative approach using game mechanics in a non-gaming context (Deterding et al. 2011). It is an interdisciplinary approach seeking to motivate users to achieve certain behavioural or psychological outcomes (e.g., learn faster, complete their personal profile, daily use of a specific platform).

A. Matallaoui · N. Hanner · R. Zarnekow (✉)
Information and Communication Management, Technical University of Berlin,
Berlin, Germany
e-mail: ruediger.zarnekow@tu-berlin.de

© Springer International Publishing Switzerland 2017
S. Stieglitz et al. (eds.), *Gamification*, Progress in IS,
DOI 10.1007/978-3-319-45557-0_1

Recent psychological studies have shown that enhancing (with game elements) information systems resulted in a significant increase of software adoption in business environments, which in turn had a positive impact on the effectiveness and efficiency of employees (Herzig et al. 2012a, b). Furthermore, gamification can lead to a change in user behaviour without resorting to extrinsic incentives such as monetary rewards or punishments. Meanwhile, gamification examples can be found in different application fields such as sustainability, environmentally conscious behaviour (Gnauk et al. 2012), enterprise resource planning, production and logistics (Herzig et al. 2012a, b) or also supporting innovation processes (Scheiner et al. 2012). Additionally, gamification has received abundant attention from research in recent years (see Fig. 1.1).

As information systems are influencing our daily routines, they are acting as a mediator that enables conveying game mechanics to users in order to motivate them to accomplish their tasks in a given context. Studies have shown that game mechanics can have a significant effect on motivation and participation in non-playful contexts (e.g., see Yang et al. 2011; Herzig et al. 2012a, b; Thom et al. 2012). Especially, latent factors such as joy, ease of use, workflow, and perceived usefulness of an application can directly be improved.

Whilst studies have shown the significant impact of game elements on user behaviour and human psychology, there is a lack of application and research for specific domains within information systems and teaching. This chapter provides the foundation for this book by introducing common concepts and theories in gamification. The section 'Foundation' provides the definition of gamification distinguishing it from gaming and game mechanics. The next section focuses on behaviour theories and models. The chapter ends with a summary.

Fig. 1.1 Published articles per year according to databases

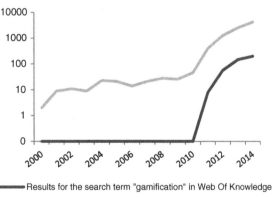

━━━ Results for the search term "gamification" in Web Of Knowledge

▒▒▒ "..." in Google Schoolar

1.2 Foundation

In this section we introduce basic foundations for this book. It includes definitions as well as the distinction between gamification and games. Additionally, we introduce game mechanics.

1.2.1 Definition

Gamification can be described as the integration of game mechanics into a non-game environment in order to give it a game-like feel (Deterding et al. 2011). The essential purpose behind designing and implementing gamification within different types of services or applications (e.g., customer-oriented applications and online services) is to increase the customer's engagement, enjoyment and also loyalty. Gamification is a relatively new term, hence there are different existing definitions.

> **Definition 1** Gamification is defined as the use of game design elements in non-game contexts (Deterding et al. 2011).

The first definition of gamification is rather general and outlines the very basic idea and supports a perhaps very common understanding of the term gamification. Yet, the potential outcomes and goals remain undefined. The concept of gamification, however, is not new and its background originates in the digital media industry (Deterding et al. 2011). Researchers and professionals have used the term *funware*, which was first defined by Zichermann and Linder (2013) as "the art and science of turning your customer's everyday interactions into games that serve your business purposes" (Zichermann and Linder 2013, p. 51). Moreover, the authors underline a potential goal of gamification as 'serving a business purpose' and suggest that gamification can indeed be used to fulfil a business purpose. In this regard another definition also explains the term gamification.

> **Definition 2** Gamification refers to a process of enhancing a service with affordances for gameful experiences in order to support user's overall value creation (Huotari and Hamari 2012).

The second definition indicates that *the use of game design elements*, here denoted as *affordances for gameful experience*, may enhance the user's experience and outcome. It also refers to the utilitarian aspect of gamification, as it should support the value creation of the user.

1.2.2 From Play to Game and Gamification

The term gamification itself first appeared in late 2010 (see Fig. 1.1) enhanced by different industry players (Deterding et al. 2011). Furthermore, as a relatively new emerging research term, gamification is still contested and many game and user experience designers have come up with other terms such as *gamefulness* and *gameful design*. Yet, it is important to distinguish between various terms that might be related or be named in the context of gamification. One of these is the distinction between playing (*paidia*) and gaming (*ludus*) as those represent two different types of activities (Caillois 1961). According to Caillois (1961), playing involves free-form, non-rule-based and expressive actions, whereas gaming represents a rule-based and goal-oriented form of playing. He defines the game concept as 'an activity that is voluntary and enjoyable, separate from the real world, uncertain, unproductive in that the activity does not produce any goods of external value, and governed by rules' (Caillois 1961). Established research theories on games and gaming consistently confirm the previous definition as they characterise *ludus* through explicit rule systems and outcomes (Salen and Zimmermann 2004; Juul 2005).

With the goal of elaborating on the previous definition of the *game* concept, McGonigal (2011) presented four fundamental features a game must have in order to fit in this classification of *ludus* and *paidia*:

- Clearly defined *goals* that provide players with a purpose for playing the game;
- Consistently defined *rules* that represent the limitations and boundaries of how to achieve the given goals;
- A steady *feedback system* that guarantees the players that the goals can be reached, if the game rules are respected;
- The *free will* of accepting participation in the game and thus following its rules to reach the goals.

It is obvious that many games come with various other features such as storytelling, interactivity or rewarding systems. However, these only form a further development and an enrichment of the basic features. Given this distinction between gaming and playing, McGonigal (2011) has subsequently introduced the concept of *gamefulness* in contrast to the term *playfulness*.

Previous research in the field of human-computer interaction (in the context of gamification) was merely dedicated to the playfulness of the existing software systems. Research focusing on the gamefulness of these systems however received less consideration despite the fact that the idea of adopting game elements in these systems was not completely new (e.g., Carroll 1982; Carrol and Thomas 1982; Malone 1982).

Gamification according to Deterding et al. (2011) is defined as the use of game design elements in non-game contexts. This definition differentiates gamification from the other related concepts by two dimensions (see Fig. 1.2). Whole versus parts refers to the extent a product or service is using gaming elements. For instance,

Fig. 1.2 Gamification, serious games, toys and playful design (Deterding et al. 2011)

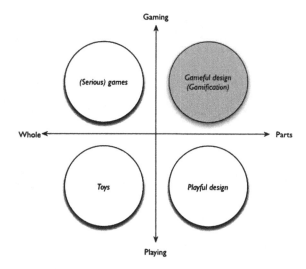

gamification differs as it only partly uses gaming elements. Other aspects of the product/service remain untouched (e.g., software can still be used to fulfil an operative task, but partly uses gaming elements to improve the enjoyment of using it) whereas serious games are complete games but may have an education or learning background (e.g., a game that teaches the problems of project management). Gaming versus playing indicates if the product/services are considering rule bound and outcome related elements (gaming) or solely comprise a playing aspect. For example, it differentiates gamification from playful design, as gamification requires a rule-based design (*you get X points by completing task X*) and a goal orientation (*get the most points*). Despite the discussed distinction between playing and gaming, practical experiences (Salen and Zimmermann 2004; Barr 2007; Groh 2011) have shown that both concepts may be integrated together and hence this separation remains somewhat theoretical.

1.2.3 Gamification Design: Game Mechanics, Dynamics and Aesthetics

In their TED talks, Chatfield (2010) and Priebatsch (2010) have presented different design principles for designing video games that, if consistently applied, may help the users engage more with the game world and better flow with the user experience it offers. They, moreover, argued that these principles can and should be applied when 'gamifying' a real-life situation to motivate the target group (e.g., enterprise employees, application users) to deal with the given tasks. The presented principles are summarily:

Fig. 1.3 MDA framework
(Hunicke et al. 2004)

- Integration and display of a progress and experience measuring component such as progression bars;
- Continuous and prompt feedback;
- Provision of long-term as well as short-term goals;
- Progressive rewarding for achieving given tasks;
- Unanticipated and non-deterministic rewarding mechanism;
- Offering a multiplayer mode (e.g., enhancing collaboration and/or challenge).

In order to apply these different fundamental principles of game and gamification design, it is important to consider the well-cited Mechanics, Dynamics and Aesthetics (MDA) framework (see Fig. 1.3) introduced by Hunicke et al. (2004). Games are defined in terms of the three concepts that form the framework.

Following the structure of the MDA framework we now introduce these concepts:

1.2.3.1 Game Mechanics

Game Mechanics describe the particular components of the game, at the level of data representation and algorithms (Hunicke et al. 2004). Game mechanics may strongly influence the user's motivation and engagement. Despite being interrelated, it is important to mention that game mechanics differ from game rules. The latter determine the endorsed behaviours that are pursued when implementing the corresponding mechanics. For example, implementing *game levels* (see below) is a game mechanic that basically allows users to level-up (e.g., upgrading the character's status) and/or level-down (e.g., downgrading Elo-rating when losing in a chess game) within a system. The behaviours/actions that cause the users to level-up or down are defined in the game rules.

The common game mechanics include:

- *Points*, which are used to reward the users through different dimensions of the system;
- *Leaderboards*, which offer users the opportunity to compare themselves to other users in the system. Despite the fact that leaderboards are generally ubiquitous, designing them is a quite delicate task since it is crucial to ensure that they encourage user behaviour instead of pushing users to abandon the given goals;
- *Levels*, which play the role of indicators showing the user's activity through the system. It is important to mention that levels do not evolve linearly and the designer could often substitute their use by integrating a badge system;

- *Achievement systems* (*AS*), which can be seen as 'meta-tasks' (tasks over key-task) that provide further goals to the system users, independently of the actual main goals. In their paper Hamari and Eranti (2011) defined achievements as follows: 'Achievements are *goals* in an *achievement/reward system* (different system than the core game) whose fulfilment is defined through activities and events in other systems (commonly in the core game)' (Hamari and Eranti 2011).

The class diagram (see Fig. 1.4) shows an adapted interpretation of a possible achievement structure presented in Hamari and Eranti (2011). Based on this diagram one can see that achievements consist mainly of three important parts, namely:

- An *identifier*, that consists of a name, through which the achievement is made unique, a description (hint) of the logic behind it and a badge, which encompasses its visualisation;
- An achievement *unlocking-logic*, which entails:
  - A *trigger*: it could be an action done by the user (e.g., eat an apple) or an event (e.g., do not smoke for a week);
  - *Conditions*: on which the trigger is based;
  - *Count*: the number of times the action or the event is triggered;
  - *Pre-requirements*: are global requirements, which have generally nothing to do with the above mentioned conditions (e.g., complexity mode should be set to hard in order to achieve this task or you need to complete badge X before you can get badge Y);

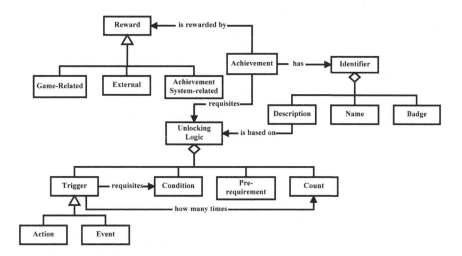

Fig. 1.4 Achievement system class diagram (Matallaoui et al. 2015)

- A *reward*, by which users are compensated for unlocking the achievement. This reward can be game-related (e.g., points), AS-related (e.g., by unlocking achievement X you fulfil one of the conditions for unlocking achievement Y) or application-external (e.g., users are rewarded with a shopping coupon).

1.2.3.2 Game Dynamics

Game dynamics describe the run-time behaviour of the mechanics acting on player inputs and each other's outputs over time (Hunicke et al. 2004). Thus, dynamics form the reason behind the user's motivational behaviour towards the game mechanics. It is crucial for game and gamification designers to target and satisfy the common desires of the different users. The common desires include (Bunchball.com 2010):

- *Rewards* are given to human beings after performing an action or showing some behaviour in order to motivate them to repeat it;
- *Status*, attention, recognition etc. are inherently needed by most humans. It is crucial for these latter to engage in some activities in order to gain the desired prestige and respect of other humans;
- *Achievement* and the need to accomplish a given task and to have goals are required by most people. Hence, people usually tend to look for new challenges and setting new achievable goals to reach;
- *Self-expression* makes it possible for people to show that they are unique and distinguishable from others;
- *Competitions* help people achieve higher levels of performance. People get motivated and satisfied when they line up and compare themselves to others;
- *Altruism* can be satisfied by making it possible for the community to give and receive gifts.

Table 1.1 shows the game mechanics that are appropriate for the different human desires. The dark points on the diagonal indicate the most suitable mechanics that satisfy the given desire (e.g., leaderboards are best used to fulfil the desire of competition among humans).

1.2.3.3 Aesthetics

Aesthetics describe the desirable emotional responses evoked in the player, when he or she interacts with the game system (Hunicke et al. 2004).

According to the MDA framework, evoking emotional responses in people (e.g., fun, surprise …) while they interact with the system enhances their motivation and engagement. According to Hunicke et al. (2004), aesthetics encompass:

Table 1.1 Human desires X game mechanics (Bunchball.com 2010)

Game Mechanics	Human Desires					
	Reward	Status	Achievement	Self Expression	Competition	Altruism
Points	●	◦	◦		◦	◦
Levels		●	◦		◦	
Challenges	◦	◦	●	◦	◦	◦
Virtual Goods	◦	◦	◦	●	◦	
Leaderboards		◦	◦		●	◦
Gifting & Charity		◦	◦		◦	●

◦ Suitablemechanic

● Most suitable mechanic

- Sensation: Game as sensory pleasure;
- Fantasy: Game as make-believe;
- Narrative: Game as drama;
- Challenge: Game as obstacle course;
- Fellowship: Game as social framework;
- Discovery: Game as uncharted territory;
- Expression: Game as self-discovery;
- Submission: Game as pastime.

Aesthetics represent a hedonic aspect of games. In the gamification context aesthetics should represent the goal of the gamified system. For example, the user feels satisfied if a task is completed by using gamified systems. Therefore, the emotional responses should not distract the user from the desired outcome. As shown in Sect. 3.4, too challenging and, therefore, frustrating game elements might diminish the user experience and take a negative toll on the user's productivity.

1.3 Gamification Underlying Theories

As mentioned in the second section, the concept of gamification is not new, and therefore it is based on different concepts and theories. Gamification can be strongly related to social science. In fact, many studies are based on well-known theories from social science like Self-Determination Theory (Ryan and Edward 2000), Job-Demand Resource Model (Demerouti et al. 2001) or Flow Theory (Csikszentmihalyi 1975; Csikszentmihalyi and LeFevre 1989). This section gives, inter alia, a closer overview of examples of theories that have tried to explain a user's behaviour and experience.

1.3.1 Motivation Theory

'Motivation is defined as the process that initiates, guides, and maintains goal-oriented behaviours. It involves the biological, emotional, social, and cognitive forces that activate behaviour' (Nevid 2012). The typical starting point for motivation theory is physiological needs. These needs can be divided into two groups: homeostasis, which refers to the body's automatic efforts to maintain a constant normal state of the blood stream, and appetites, which refers to giving our body what it needs (Maslow 1943).

1.3.2 Extrinsic Versus Intrinsic Motivation

Different types of motivation are generally described as being either extrinsic or intrinsic (Nevid 2012):

- Extrinsic motivations are motivations that come from outside of the individual and often involve external rewards such as trophies, money, social recognition or praise;
- Intrinsic motivations are motivations that originate from within (inside) the individual, such as trying to solve a puzzle purely for the self-gratification of solving that puzzle.

In addition to these two general types of motivation, users usually follow and show different, more particular motives for conducting given actions. Next, we provide an introduction to the different user types and their motivations.

1.3.3 Player Types

Bartle (1996) defined four different archetypes of video game players, which also represent various kinds of motivations the players may have. Various education and learning-related works (Kim and Ko 2013; Hawlitschek and Köppen 2014a, b; Liu and Liu 2005) have for instance been based on Bartle's categorisation. It is important to mention that it is unlikely to find one single user representing exactly one single type; most users commonly represent more than one type. It is also typical for users to alternate between different archetypes throughout their learning experiences. These types are described by Bartle (1996) as:

- *Killers* represent competitive users who enjoy challenging other users and winning against them. Triumphing is the key goal killers pursue;
- *Achievers* characterise the type of users whose main incentive is to accumulate points, to level up and to get higher rankings;

Fig. 1.5 Bartle's player types (Bartle 1996)

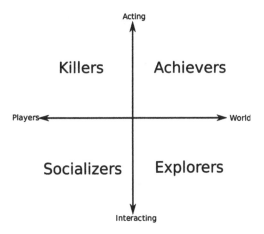

- *Socialisers* represent the kind of users who use the application as a bridge to get in contact with other users and to interact with them. The community is a vital stimulus for the users of this type;
- *Explorers* represent the type of users who want to discover the application as well as its boundaries. Exploring the application is the user's main drive.

Bartle projected the mentioned archetypes onto the diagram illustrated in Fig. 1.5. The figure should be read as follows:

- Killers act on other players;
- Achievers act on the world;
- Socialisers interact with other players;
- Explorers interact with the world.

1.3.4 Achievement Goal Theory

One of the recent and growing features in gamified systems and serious games is the introduction of AS. These systems form a meta-game that provides the target group with additional goals that are independent of the main goals. On account of this, gamification designers have theorised that these meta-games may be an important means for enhancing the user's engagement. They, however, had to be cleverly integrated and categorised in order to achieve the pursued behaviour.

Based on Galli and Fraternali (2014) and considering the different player types we introduced above (see section Player Types), we list the different types of achievements:

- **Instructors** are used to guide the users through the learning process. They ensure that given actions are mastered by the users so that they can be used to progress with the learning experience. The advantages of providing such achievements include encouraging the users to understand and interact with the system as well as motivating them right from the start to get the needed knowledge and skills (e.g., going through on-board tutorials).

- **Quests** are unlocked when users, for instance, accomplish significant tasks. A quest is usually awarded once when its required conditions are fulfilled for the first time. The key goal for having such achievements is to continuously keep users involved.
- **Content Discovery** achievements encourage users to explore the application. They ensure that the users are at least aware of all the existing modes and features the application is offering and have gone through them.
- **Socialiser** achievements are awarded when users undertake certain tasks within the community. This type of achievement encourages collaborative learning and thus enhances the overall performance of the users.
- **Grinder** achievements are unlocked when a task is repeated a given number of times. They represent an easy to implement type of achievement and are deployed to entice users to master particular actions, which are considered crucial for further use of the application.
- **Herculean Tasks** represent a type of achievement awarded when users accomplish relatively difficult and hard to perform tasks. These achievements, requiring decent skills, can be as a matter of course unlocked only by experienced users.
- **Trophies** are only awarded to a few users in the community, since they are designed to mutually exclude other users from winning them.
- **Loyalty** achievements are awarded to users who in fact show loyalty towards the application. Although inciting users to spend real money on the game, this type of achievement is particularly considered by the application community.

1.3.5   User Experience: Flow Theory

Flow theory is based on the notion of positive psychology, which mainly focuses on intrinsic strengths. Seligman and Csikszentmihalyi (2000) defined it as "the study of positive emotion, positive character, and positive institutions." Csikszentmihalyi, as one of the pioneers in the field of positive psychology, was captivated by the fact that some people, despite their tremendous losses during the war, were still happy and showed their happiness while others could not. It was then that he produced the Flow Theory (see Fig. 1.6) by treating happiness as a *positive, personal state of being* (Whitson and Consoli 2009).

Csikszentmihalyi (2008) defined happiness in the context of accomplishing a task as not getting bored on the one hand and not feeling anxious on the other hand. He further stated that Flow Theory can be seen as a theory of optimal experience based on the concept of flow—the state in which people are so involved in an

Fig. 1.6 Flow theory
(Csikszentmihalyi 2008)

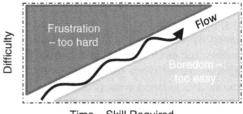

Time – Skill Required

activity that nothing else seems to matter. The experience itself is so enjoyable that people will do it even at great cost, for the sheer sake of doing it (Csikszentmihalyi 2008).

Csikszentmihalyi (2008) identified different characteristics of flow. The ones that are directly related to motivation and engagement and should be taken into consideration when designing gamification are:

- A challenging activity that requires skills;
- Merging of action and awareness;
- Concentration on the task at hand;
- Clear goals and feedback.

1.4 Summary

This introductory chapter has shown that gamification has become an emerging concept in research. Results from various studies supported the idea that the application of gamification could significantly influence the efficiency of human work and the enjoyment of executing it. Therefore, gamification can be applied in many contexts, as it partly introduces game elements into a product or a service. It is important to mention that gamification does not require the gamified product or service to turn into a complete *game*. Consequently, we introduced two definitions of gamification which represent different perspectives in terms of application and outcomes. These definitions revealed that just *gamifying* a system would not be meaningful if the wanted goals, the desired outcomes and the utilitarian task that should be completed have not been set and clearly defined. To achieve these goals, mechanics, dynamics and aesthetics play an important role (Hawlitschek and Köppen 2014a, b). Game mechanics represent the design possibilities and mechanisms that allow integrating game elements into a specific non-gaming context. Game mechanics are probably the most significant part of gamification, since leaderboards, points and AS are the primary features of a gamified system. Yet, only under the consideration of game dynamics and aesthetics could the game mechanics be shaped and used in a meaningful way to achieve changes in human behaviour including increasing motivation and further engagement. Under the section 'Gamification Underlying Theories', we provided a closer look at examples of given theories that have tried to explain a user's behaviour and experience. We started by briefly introducing the motivation theory and distinguished between intrinsic and extrinsic motivation. Subsequently, we provided an introduction to the different player types (Bartle 1996) revealing how human motivation and their actions in a gameful context can be classified according to various kinds of motivations these players may have. Finally, we introduced Flow Theory and outlined different achievement types, which form a meta-game that provides the target group with additional goals that are independent of the main goals and thus act as motivators to accomplish the latter.

References

Barr, P. (2007). Video game values: Play as human-computer interaction. *Interacting with Computers, 19*(2), 180–195.

Bartle, R. (1996). Hearts, clubs, diamonds, spades: players who suit MUDs. *Journal of MUD Research, 1*(1), 19.

Bunchball.com. (2010, 10). *Gamification 101: An Introduction to the Use of Game Dynamics to Influence Behavior*. Retrieved from http://www.bunchball.com/sites/default/files/downloads/gamification101.pdf

Caillois, R. (1961). *Man, play and games*. Chicago: University of Illinois Press.

Carroll, J. M. (1982). The adventure of getting to know a computer. *Computer, 15*(11), 49–58.

Chatfield, T. (2010, 7). *Tom Chatfield: 7 Ways Games Reward the Brain*. Retrieved from TED Talks: http://www.ted.com/talks/tom_chatfield_7_ways_games_reward_the_brain.html

Csikszentmihalyi, M. (1975). *Beyond boredom and anxiety: Experiencing flow in work and play*. San Francisco: Jossey-Bass.

Csikszentmihalyi, M. (2008). *Flow: The psychology of optimal experience*. New York: HarperCollins.

Csikszentmihalyi, M., & LeFevre, J. (1989). Optimal experience in work and leisure. *Journal of Personality and Social Psychology, 56*(5), 815–822.

Demerouti, E., Bakker, A., Nachreiner, F., & Schaufeli, W. (2001). The job demands-resources model of burnout. *Journal of Applied Psychology, 6*(3), 499–512.

Deterding, S., Dixon, D., Khaled, R., & Nacke, L. (2011). From game design elements to gamefulness: Defining gamification. In *MindTrek '11 Proceedings of the 15th International Academic MindTrek Conference: Envisioning Future Media Environments* (pp. 9–15). ACM.

Galli, L., & Fraternali, P. (2014). Achievement systems explained. In Y. Baek, R. Ko, & T. Marsh (Eds.), *Trends and applications of serious gaming and social media* (pp. 22–50). Singapore: Springer.

Gnauk, B., Dannecker, L., & Hahmann, B. (2012). Leveraging gamification in demand dispatch systems. In *EDBT-ICDT '12 Proceedings of the 2012 Joint EDBT/ICDT Workshops* (pp. 103–110).

Groh, F. (2011). Gamification: State of the art definition and utilization. In N. Asaj, B. Könings, M. Poguntke, F. Schaub, B. Wiedersheim, & M. Weber (Eds.), *Proceedings of the 4th Seminar on Research Trends in Media Informatics* (pp. 39–45).

Hamari, J., & Eranti, V. (2011). Framework for designing and evaluating game achievements. In *DiGRA '11—Proceedings of the 2011 DiGRA International Conference: Think Design Play* (Vol. 6, pp. 122–134).

Hawlitschek, A., & Köppen, V. (2014a). Analyzing player behavior in digital game-based learning: Advantages and challenges. In *The 8th European Conference on Games Based Learning—ECGBL*. Berlin.

Hawlitschek, A., & Köppen, V. (2014b). Analyzing player behavior in digital game-based learning: Advantages and challenges. In *Proceedings of the European Conference on Games Based Learning* (Vol. 1, p. 199).

Herzig, P., Ameling, M., & Schill, A. (2012a). A generic platform for enerprise gamification. In *10th Working IEEE/IFIP Conference on Software Architecture*, (pp. 219–223).

Herzig, P., Srahringer, S., & Ameling, M. (2012b). Gamification of ERP systems—Exploring gamification effects on user acceptance constructs. In *Multikonferenz Wirtschaftsinformatik GITO* (pp. 793–804).

Huizinga, J. (1949). *Homo Ludens a study of the play-element in culture*. London: Routledge & Kegan Paul.

Hunicke, R., LeBlanc, M., & Zubek, R. (2004). MDA: A formal approach to game design and game research. In *Proceedings of the Challenges in Games AI Workshop, Nineteenth National Conference on Artificial Intelligence*. San Jose, CA.

Huotari, K., & Hamari, J. (2012). Defining gamification: A service marketing perspective. In *International Academic MindTrek Conference* (pp. 17–22). New York, USA.

Juul, J. (2005). *Half-real: Video games between rules and fictional worlds*. MIT Press

Kim, S., & Ko, F. (2013). Toward gamified classroom: Classification of engineering students based on the Bartle's player types model. *International Journal of Digital Content Technology and its Applications (JDCTA), 7*(2), 25.

Liu, Z., & Liu, Z. (2005). Building an intelligent pedagogical agent with competiton mechanism to improve the effectiveness of an educational game. In *Workshop on educational games as intelligent learning environments*.

Malone, T. W. (1982). Heursitics for designing enjoyable user interfaces: Lessons from computer games. In *Proceedings of the Conference on Human Factors in Computer Systems* (pp. 63–86). New York.

Maslow, A. H. (1943). A theory of human motivation. *Psychological Review, 50*(4), 370–396.

Matallaoui, A., Herzig, P., & Zarnekow, R. (2015). Model-Driven serious game development: Integration of the gamification modeling language GaML with unity. In *48th Hawaii International Conference on System Sciences (HICSS)* (pp. 643–651). IEEE.

McGonigal, J. (2011). *Reality is broken: Why games make us better and how they can change the world*. New York: Penguin.

Nevid, J. (2012). *Psychology: Concepts and applications* (4th ed.). Belmont, CA: Wadworth: Cengage Learning.

Priebatsch, S. (2010, 8). *Seth Priebatsch: The game layer on top of the world*. Retrieved from TED Talks: http://www.ted.com/talks/seth_priebatsch_the_game_layer_on_top_of_the_world.html

Ryan, R. M., & Edward, D. L. (2000). Self-determination theory and the facilitation of intrinsic motivation, social development, and well-being. *American Psychologist, 55*, 68–78.

Salen, K., & Zimmermann, E. (2004). *Rules of play: Game design fundamentals*. : MIT Press.

Scheiner, C., Witt, M., Voigt, K., & Robra-Bissantz, S. (2012). Einsatz von Spielemechaniken in Ideewettbewerben. In *Multikonferenz Wirtschaftsinformatik* (pp. 781–792).

Seligman, M., & Csikszentmihalyi, M. (2000). Positive psychology: An introduction. *American Psycholigist, 55*(1), 5–14.

Thom, J., Millen, D., & DiMicco, J. (2012). Removing Gamification from an Enterprise SNS. In *CSCW '12 Proceedings of the ACM 2012 conference on Computer Supported Cooperative Work* (pp. 1067–1070).

Thomas, J. M. (1982). Metaphor and the cognitive representation of computing systems. *IEEE Transactions on Systems, Man, and Cybernetics, 12*(2), 107–116.

Whitson, C., & Consoli, J. (2009). Flow theory and student engagement. *Journal of Cross-Disciplinary Perspectives in Education, 2*(1), 40–49.

Yang, J., Ackerman, M. S., Adamic, & A. L. (2011). Virtual Gifts and Guanxi: Supporting Social Exchange in a Chinese Online Community. In *CSCW '11 Proceedings of the ACM 2011 conference on Computer supported cooperative work* (pp. 45–54).

Zichermann, G., & Linder, J. (2013). *The gamification revolution: How leaders leverage game mechanics to crush the competition* (1st ed.). USA: McGraw-Hill Education.

Chapter 2
Gamification and Behaviour

**Alaa AlMarshedi, Vanissa Wanick, Gary B. Wills
and Ashok Ranchhod**

Abstract Gamification is applied as a tool to encourage behavioural change and promote desired attitudes in many fields. However, people with different backgrounds are influenced by gamification in different ways. This suggests that cultural influence can also impact the way gamification is best implemented within a particular context. This chapter starts by discussing how behaviour can be influenced by gamification. It then considers how culture in its different manifestations influences behaviour. The chapter then discusses motivation and its role in gamification. Finally, the key issue of the behavioural change capabilities of gamification combined with an understanding of behavioural change methods, the individual and the cultural and social context are discussed.

2.1 Introduction

Gamification is a design process that applies play, fun and user experience elements to different applications/services in non-gaming contexts (Deterding et al. 2011). Since gamification is a relatively new area, many of the current approaches focus on the gaming elements. To just concentrate on gaming elements would be wrong as a large aspect of gamification is about psychological issues (Zichermann and Cunningham 2011). This means that to get the most out of gamification and its

A. AlMarshedi · G.B. Wills
School of Electronics and Computer Science, University of Southampton,
Southampton SO17 1BJ, UK
e-mail: aaa3g12@ecs.soton.ac.uk

G.B. Wills
e-mail: gbw@ecs.soton.ac.uk

V. Wanick (✉) · A. Ranchhod
Winchester School of Art, University of Southampton, Winchester SO23 8DL, UK
e-mail: v.w.vieira@soton.ac.uk

A. Ranchhod
e-mail: a.ranchhod@soton.ac.uk

© Springer International Publishing Switzerland 2017
S. Stieglitz et al. (eds.), *Gamification*, Progress in IS,
DOI 10.1007/978-3-319-45557-0_2

application in business, education, or healthcare, the behaviour of an individual and the cultural context need to be understood. Often concepts from cultural psychology are incorporated into games to influence consumer behaviour and alter particular behaviour patterns in areas such as healthcare and education. Consumer behaviour is the relationship between the user and the applications/services that are being offered or have been purchased. This includes individual or collective attributes, emotional attachments, communications understanding and decision-making (Britt 1966). Moreover, this behaviour is often tempered by cultural nuances and these may vary across cultures (Usunier and Lee 2005). Therefore, actions that involve behavioural change do not occur in a vacuum. At the same time, differences between individuals and groups in gamification need to be studied, particularly in different cultures as there are certain cultural norms that can further affect gamification's effectiveness. Some studies have considered age and gender (Koivisto and Hamari 2014), however, culture has rarely been examined.

This chapter discusses theories and methods that are part of gamification. It includes a discussion of the application of gamification for behaviour change, together with an understanding of the differences and similarities across cultures. Cultural dimensions and social aspects in gamification are also considered. The knowledge about individual behaviour and the incorporation of cross-cultural differences could potentially enhance gamification's impact in different fields.

2.2 Influencing Behaviour

One of gamification's goals is to influence a user's behaviour. It shares some similarities with persuasive technology: technologies that are designed to influence a user's behaviour without forcing the change (Hamari et al. 2014). Moreover, behaviour change is the process in which an undesired behaviour is abandoned in favour of a better one. There are some methods and theories to assist in changing the behaviour of an individual or a community (N.I.C.E. 2007). Moreover, it has been proven that online behavioural change methods are successful in influencing user's behaviours (Cugelman et al. 2011).

In order to influence behaviour, we need to understand how behaviour is created and what affects behaviour. This includes behavioural change methods (interventions to affect an individual) as well as cultural and social influences.

2.2.1 Motivation

Motivation is an important factor to consider in gamification (Nicholson 2012), particularly because it drives human behaviour (Xu 2012). Several studies investigating motivation and behaviour have been carried out throughout history, and we have a number of theories that explain motivation and how it affects behaviour.

Motivation is the desire to do something and it could be explained in two ways: intrinsic and extrinsic. Intrinsic motivation is defined by an internal desire to do things out of enjoyment or love (Ryan and Deci 2000). On the other hand, extrinsic motivation is about doing things solely for their outcome (Ryan and Deci 2000).

The understanding of how behaviour is created is crucial in the design of gamification applications and services. This helps in creating effective gamification that can influence consumer behaviour, changing behaviour in healthcare situations and learning. A number of gamified applications and services today focus on motivation, especially the extrinsic type (Sudan 2013). However, extrinsic motivation by itself does not create a sustainable gamification affect (Koivisto and Hamari 2014). Thus, understanding the difference between extrinsic motivation and intrinsic motivation is important when designing gamified applications and services.

In gamification, motivation is used to start an activity. When users perform a task they might realise the intrinsic value of this activity and might want to do it without rewards or extrinsic motivations. It is important to mention that tangible rewards or extrinsic motivation cannot be used as the only way to change behaviour. This is because extrinsic motivation can wax and wane depending on individual characteristics (Hamari et al. 2014). Thus, change in behaviour could be temporary before the individual reverts to his/her original behaviour. For example, while individuals feel motivated to exercise and look for positive outcomes, they may lose the desire for these outcomes over the course of time. Thus, an individual's behaviour reverts to its original state and the behaviour change results are lost.

2.3 Cultural Influences

Culture has many definitions and it shapes people's responses and preferences for computer systems and communications. For example, Hofstede (1997) defined culture as a system of patterns that differentiates people of one group from the other. Usunier and Lee (2005) argued that culture is a combination of shared habits and meanings, interpreted within a particular context. The context and environment shape different cultures.

A few aspects of consumer behaviour are influenced by culture: perception, motivation, learning and memory, group influence, social class, female/male roles, attitudes and decision-making (Usunier and Lee 2005). The result of this is a very complex set of variables that need to be understood in the field of consumer behaviour. Considering individuals from different cultures, consumer values and needs can differ and influence behaviour differently. For example, individuals from China can place more value on experiential characteristics while buying clothes, whereas South Korean individuals may desire functional product features (e.g., product quality) (Kim et al. 2002).

Furthermore, habits play an important role in culture, as they facilitate choices during everyday life decisions (Usunier and Lee 2005). This means that habits could be immersed within social contexts such as social habits. In addition, decision-making can be grounded on behavioural biases, based on heuristics or mental models (Hamari et al. 2015). This means that the consideration of behavioural and cultural patterns is crucial for an effective application of gamification in consumer behaviour. Hence, it is possible that cultural biases could guide users in the decision process when interacting with gamified applications.

Cultural models and dimensions have been mentioned before in order to investigate cross-cultural differences in several applications (Khaled 2015; Chakraborty and Norcio 2009).

Concisely, cultural dimensions and models can be summarised as follows:

- Hofstede's (2011) cultural dimensions: Power Dimension, related to the degree of how well a society understands inequalities among people; Individualism vs. Collectivism, represented specifically by an individual or collective way to see relationships in society; Masculinity versus Femininity, related to preferences among achievement, rewards, competition and cooperation; Uncertainty Avoidance, describing the way society deals with the future; Pragmatic vs. Normative (e.g., in normative cultures, people usually explain things as much as possible, while in pragmatic cultures situations, context and time are more important); Indulgence vs. Restraint, related to enjoyment of life and social norms that regulate society.
- Trompenaars and Hampden-Turner's (1998) dimensions: Universalism-Particularism (e.g., for Universalist cultures, rules are more important than relationships), Individualism-Communitarianism (individual-group relationship), Specific-Diffuse (related to involvement), Neutral-Emotional (e.g., expression of emotions, body language and attitudes), Achievement-Ascription (related to status), Sequential Time-Synchronous Time (time management), and Internal Direction-Outer Direction (connection and link to the control of the environment).
- Hall's (1989) four cultural categories in communication: Time (e.g., time management), Space (e.g., personal or shared spaces); Context (e.g., explicit and direct messages vs. implicit and indirect messages); Information Flow (e.g., message speed).
- Schwartz's (2006) structures of individual values (e.g., benevolence, tradition, security, power, achievement, hedonism, stimulation, self-direction and universalism), which correspond with seven national-level value types (e.g., egalitarianism, harmony, embeddedness, hierarchy, mastery, intellectual autonomy and affective autonomy).

The list of Hofstede's (2011) cultural dimensions is usually used in comparisons across cultural aspects in different nations. The spectrum between individualism and collectivism has been one of the most explored areas within cultural research. In general, individualist cultures tend to have an independent view of the self and collectivist cultures have an interdependent view of the self (Aaker and Maheswaran 1997).

In gamified applications/services, culture could also influence the way people relate to each other. Specifically, Khaled (2015) presented at least six components of relationships between people enhanced by gamified applications/services, such as competition, information sharing, normative activities, interdependence and sense of community. Moreover, Khaled (2015) utilised Schwartz's (2006) model as a starting point, supporting the argument that people from different cultures tend to have different psychological beliefs and this could be expressed by dynamics promoted by gamified applications/services.

When considering cultural aspects and gaming, there are at least three classifications to explore: appropriation, cultural representations and the creation of subcultures (Khaled 2015). Culture and design could be combined to create serious games. For example, cultural appropriation could be employed in order to support the game's mechanics, storyline and interface by designers from a different culture (Vasalou et al. 2014). This strategy could also be also associated with representational variations amongst different cultures by using a diverse range of colours, icons, symbols, pictures, time formats, jargon and abbreviations (Bourges-Waldegg and Scrivener 1998).

Furthermore, considering culture and interactive systems, other theories and applications could be expanded, such as:

- Semiotics: the study of signs and symbolic representations as references to a particular idea (Pierce 1991). For example, in gamification, semiotics could be used as a way to build the bridge between the desired behaviour and the actual behaviour, respecting people's abilities to understand the codes of the system.
- Symbolic interactionism: the understanding of meanings as products from social activities, in which people's actions, norms and rules comprise the concept of culture (Blumer 1986). For example, the study of gamified applications could be expanded to the meaning that people give to systems during their interaction and experience.
- Metaphors: related to analogies or familiarity (Carroll and Thomas 1982). This is consistent with the principle that before performing a task, users try to find connections in their mind and associative memory (Lang 2006). For example, the replication of metaphors inside the gamified system could make the application more intuitive and easy to understand. Those metaphors could be visual or interactive representations, depending on the audience and on the objective of the gamified system.

The possibilities for the incorporation and study of culture and gamification are vast. However, as members of a group often share cultural values within a context, it is important to open the discussion to social factors and influences.

2.4 Social Influences

Social factors could also influence behaviour through social norms (Ajzen and Fishbein 1980; Ajzen 1991). For example, people and communities are often ruled by norms through which members behave in a particular way, influencing their opinion adoption (Hsu and Lu 2004). In addition, social behaviour can differ across cultures, particularly in high individualist cultures where individuals behave socially according to personal preferences (Aaker and Maheswaran 1997).

At least four models incorporate social and environmental influences in behavioural studies:

- Theory of Reasoned Action (TRA) (Ajzen and Fishbein 1980): Intentions are formed because of attitudes, norms and perceived control over individual behaviour.
- Theory of Planned Behaviour (TPB) (Ajzen 1991): An extension of the Theory of Reasoned Action (TRA) that includes the variable of perceived control over the behaviour (i.e., perception that someone is responsible for his/her behaviour).
- Needs, Opportunity and Ability Model (NOA) (Gatersleben and Vlek 1998): The environment, comprising technology, economy, demography, institutions and culture, influences needs, opportunities and abilities, which therefore impact motivation and behavioural control. This model expands cultural influences to a wider level, such as government politics.
- Theory of Interpersonal Behaviour (TIB) (Triandis 1977): The relationship among attitudes, contextual factors, personal capabilities and habits. This model contributes by emphasising the role of beliefs and habits on behaviour.

Compared to Fogg's (2009) model of behaviour, where he discusses *motivation*, *ability*, and *trigger* as behavioural components, the TIB, TRA, TPB and NOA tend to integrate social and external influences (e.g., environment, norms and laws) into behaviour design. For this reason, it is possible that Fogg's behavioural model could be combined with social, cultural and external factors. In gamification, this could be another way to provide a holistic and inclusive experience for the user.

2.5 Behaviour Change Theories and Methods

To influence a user's behaviour, one must understand how behaviour occurs and what contributes to it. Fogg (2009) proposed a model that explains how behaviour occurs. The Fogg Behaviour Model (FBM) shows that human behaviour is an outcome of three elements. The first element is *motivation*, which describes when the person has the desire to act in a certain way. The second element is *ability*, which describes when the person has the capacity to perform the behaviour. The last element is *trigger*, which describes when the person is triggered to perform the behaviour through different cues. Fogg (2009) stated that these elements must happen at the same time in order for behaviour to result.

Furthermore, influencing behaviours is a two-step procedure (Wu 2014). It requires both, creating a new behaviour and eliminating the undesired habit. There are a number of situations where people are internally motivated to change their behaviour. On the other hand, behaviour change could result from self-realisation, change in environment, or developing a new behaviour through a sequence of steps. The latter is called 'Tiny Habits' where a planned sequence of small changes in daily routine results in the adoption of tiny habits to reach a desired behaviour (Fogg 2013). The Tiny Habit method has been shown to be successful in changing behaviour (Fogg 2011). It relies on the fact that small changes are easier to accept than big shifts in daily behaviour.

The 'Flow State' is the mental state of absorption and engagement in an activity or a game (Csikszentmihalyi 1997). In this state, the user becomes intrinsically motivated and immersed in the activity. In order to get the user into the flow state the game must be compatible with the user's skill level. One way of achieving this is by gradually increasing the difficulty of each task/level as the user's skills increase (Cugelman 2013), which ensures the sustainability of the flow state. If the game is too simple the user will get bored, and if it is too difficult the user may quit.

Additionally, Pink (2009) maintained that motivation is intrinsic and it is driven by three elements: *autonomy*, *mastery*, and *purpose*. *Autonomy* occurs when people have full control over when and to what level they want to carry out the activity. In games, one of the components of autonomy is entering the flow state. *Mastery* is about getting better at a certain activity. For example, a sense of mastery can be reached through improvement in playing and progressing towards goals (McGonigal 2011). The final element *purpose* is when people have a reason to do an activity. Furthermore, *status* is another powerful motivator because people care about their image (Ariely et al. 2009). One example of this is the use of badges and leaderboards that indicate how a person is performing relative to others.

One of the theories known to drive behaviour is the Nudge Theory. It is the positive reinforcement and indirect signals toward a non-forced action. Nudge Theory is used to drive behaviour and it has been applied in political and economical environments (Thaler and Sunstien 2009). It creates the simplest path to a certain behaviour. The use of Nudge Theory could create a good environment combined with gamification: giving rewards and incentives as well as 'nudging' users into wanted behaviours. Moreover, Wu (2011) argued that gamification in its simplest form covers the *motivation* element in FBM, and the Nudge Theory covers the two other elements, *ability* and *trigger*. Designing a nudge is similar to designing a tiny habit: it has to be simple choices. However, the Nudge Theory requires the designer to simplify the environment and the context that leads to a certain action. On the other hand, the tiny habits method breaks down the desired behaviour into easy-to-adopt small habits.

Figure 2.1 summarises the key influences in a user's behaviour in gamification and how changing the extrinsic motivation through the attention to social and cultural issues could enact behaviour change.

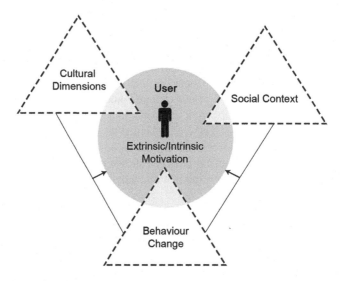

Fig. 2.1 Drivers of motivation in gamification

2.6 Discussion and Conclusion

Gamification is more psychology than technology and the development of motivation is an important factor to consider. Motivation, which is the desire to perform an action, can be intrinsic or extrinsic. Intrinsic motivation is the internal desire to do things out of enjoyment or love, while extrinsic motivation occurs when one is doing things solely for an outcome. One of gamification's goals is to drive a user's behaviour. In gamification, both types of motivators should be used to create a lasting effect, and keep the user interested in the activity. In order to change or influence behaviour through gamification, it is important to understand how behaviours occur and what motivates them. A number of theories and methods explain the nature of behaviour and how behaviours occur. Fogg, Pink, and Thaler and Sunstein created methods and processes that help in changing behaviour of an individual or a community. Fogg created the FBM, which suggested that behaviour is an outcome of three elements: *motivation, ability*, and *trigger*. According to the model, the three elements must occur simultaneously for a particular behaviour to occur. He also suggested the use of 'Tiny Habits' methods, in which a planned sequence of small changes in a person's daily routine results in the adoption of tiny habits to reach a desired behaviour. Pink argued that motivation is intrinsic and driven by three elements: autonomy, mastery, and purpose. Thaler and Sunstien's theory, called the Nudge Theory, entails positive reinforcement and indirect signals toward a non-forced action.

Furthermore, the opportunities for implementations of gamification in innovative ways are vast. The consideration of cultural patterns and behavioural biases is crucial for the development of innovation in businesses. For this reason, it is important to highlight the possibilities of studies in cross-cultural consumer behaviour. The literature of consumer behaviour across cultures looks for an explanation of the differences and similarities of people from different backgrounds in their decision-making process. This aspect tends to be reflected in the way cognitive patterns and mental models are processed by the users. However, in cross-cultural consumer behaviour it is possible that culture could be explained through different cultural models and dimensions combined with the meaning that people give to particular applications/services.

Gamification and culture can be explored in two ways: one from the perspective of interaction with the product or system, and the other from the cultural values already planned and enhanced by the design of the system. The consideration of patterns in cultural backgrounds is an important way to help predict consumer behaviour while using gamification in services. Furthermore, strategies such as semiotics and symbolic interactionism could help to identify those patterns and models of behaviour. On the other hand, it is necessary to consider the influence that the social background has in the individual's behaviours; Khaled (2015) argued that interpersonal dynamics are crucial for understanding culture and gamification.

For future research in gamification, we suggest that the cultural dimensions applied in different fields and the methods borrowed from interactive systems could be studied in relation to the application of gamification. This includes semiotics, conceptual metaphors and symbolic interactionism.

Acknowledgments Alaa AlMarshedi gratefully acknowledges the sponsorship by King Abdullah Foreign Scholarship Program, Saudi Arabia. Vanissa Wanick gratefully acknowledges the grant from Coordenação de Aperfeiçoamento de Pessoal de Nível Superior (CAPES), Brazil, (number: 9520-13-9). The authors would like to thank James Baker, who kindly provided proofreading comments.

References

Aaker, J. L., & Maheswaran, D. (1997). The effect of cultural orientation on persuasion. *Journal of Consumer Research, 24*(3), 315–328. doi:10.1086/209513

Ajzen, I., & Fishbein, M. (1980). *Understanding attitudes and predicting social behaviour.* Englewood-Cliffs, NJ: Prentice-Hall.

Ajzen, I. (1991). The theory of planned behaviour. *Organisational Behaviour and Human Decision Processes, 50*, 179–211. doi:10.1016/0749-5978(91)90020-T

Ariely, D., Bracha, A., & Meier, S. (2009). Doing good or doing well? Image motivation and monetary incentives in behaving prosocially. *The American Economic Review, 99*(1), 544–555. doi:10.1257/aer.99.1.544

Blumer, H. (1986). *Symbolic interactionism: Perspective and method.* University of California Press.

Bourges-Waldegg, P., & Scrivener, S. A. (1998). Meaning, the central issue in cross-cultural HCI design. *Interacting with Computers, 9*(3), 287–309. doi:10.1016/S0953-5438(97)00032-5

Britt, S. H. (1966). *Consumer behaviour and the behavioural sciences: Theories and applications.* Oxford, England: John Wiley & Sons.

Carroll, J. M., & Thomas, J. C. (1982). Metaphor and the cognitive representation of computing systems. *IEEE Transactions on Systems, Man, and Cybernetics, 12*(2), 107–116. doi:10.1109/TSMC.1982.4308795

Chakraborty, J., & Norcio, A. F. (2009). Cross cultural computer gaming. In *Internationalization, Design and Global Development* (pp. 13–18). doi:10.1007/978-3-642-02767-3_2

Csikszentmihalyi, M. (1997). *Finding flow: The psychology of engagement with everyday life.* Basic Books.

Cugelman, B. (2013). Gamification: What it is and why it matters to digital health behaviour change developers. *JMIR Serious Games, 1*(1). doi:10.2196/games.3139

Cugelman, B., Thelwall, M., & Dawes, P. (2011). Online interventions for social marketing health behaviour change campaigns: A meta-analysis of psychological architectures and adherence factors. *Journal of Medical Internet Research, 13*(1). doi:10.2196/jmir.1367

Deterding, S., et al. (2011). From game design elements to gamefulness. In: *Proceedings of the 15th International Academic MindTrek Conference on Envisioning Future Media Environments—MindTrek '11* (p. 9). New York, New York, USA: ACM Press.

Fogg, B. J. (2009). A behaviour model for persuasive design. In *Proceedings of the 4th International Conference on Persuasive Technology.* doi:10.1145/1541948.1541999

Fogg, B. J. (2011). Tiny Habits w/ Dr. BJ Fogg- Behaviour Change. Tiny Habits. http://tinyhabits.com/. Accessed November 18, 2014.

Fogg, B. J. (2013). Fogg Method. Fogg Method: 3 steps to changing behaviour. http://www.foggmethod.com/. Accessed December 27, 2014.

Gatersleben, B., & Vlek, C. (1998). Household consumption, quality of life and environmental impacts. In K. J. Noorman, A. J. M. Schoot-Uiterkamp (Eds.), *Green households? Domestic consumers, environment and sustainability* (pp. 141–183). London: Earthscan.

Hall, E. T. (1989). *Beyond culture.* New York: Anchor Books.

Hamari, J., Huotari, K., & Tolvanen, J. (2015). Gamification and economics. In S. Waltz & S. Deterding (Eds.), *The gameful world: Approaches, issues, applications* (pp. 139–162). Cambridge: MIT Press.

Hamari, J., Koivisto, J., & Pakkanen, T. (2014a). Do persuasive technologies persuade? A review of empirical studies. In *Persuasive Technology* (pp. 118–136). doi:10.1007/978-3-319-07127-5_11

Hamari, J., Koivisto, J., & Sarsa, H. (2014b). Does gamification work? A literature review of empirical studies on gamification. In *47th Hawaii International Conference on System Sciences* (pp. 3025–3034). doi:10.1109/hicss.2014.377

Hofstede, G. (2011). Dimensionalizing cultures: The Hofstede model in context. *Online Readings in Psychology and Culture, 2*(1), 8. doi:10.9707/2307-0919.1014

Hofstede, G. (1997). *Cultures and organizations.* New York, NY: McGraw Hill.

Hsu, C.-L., & Lu, H.-P. (2004). Why do people play on-line games? An extended TAM with social influences and flow experience. *Information & Management, 41*(7), 853–868. doi:10.1016/j.im.2003.08.014

Khaled, R. (2015). Gamification and culture. In S. Waltz & S. Deterding (Eds.), *The gameful world: Approaches, issues, applications* (pp. 301–322). Cambridge: MIT Press.

Kim, J. O., Forsythe, S., Gu, Q., & Moon, S. J. (2002). Cross-cultural consumer values, needs and purchase behaviour. *Journal of Consumer Marketing, 19*(6), 481–502. doi:10.1108/07363760210444869

Koivisto, J., & Hamari, J. (2014). Demographic differences in perceived benefits from gamification. *Computers in Human Behaviour, 35*, 179–188. doi:10.1016/j.chb.2014.03.007

Lang, A. (2006). Using the limited capacity model of motivated mediated message processing to design effective cancer communication messages. *Journal of Communication, 56*, S57–S80. doi:10.1111/j.1460-2466.2006.00283.x

McGonigal, J. (2011). *Reality is broken: Why games make us better and how they can change the world.* Penguin Books.

N.I.C.E. (2007). *Behaviour change: The principles for effective interventions.* NICE. http://www.nice.org.uk/guidance/ph6. Accessed December 15, 2014.

Nicholson, S. (2012). A user-centered theoretical framework for meaningful gamification. In *Games Learning Society 8.0*.

Peirce, C. S. (1991). Peirce on signs: Writings on semiotic. UNC Press Books.

Pink, D. (2009). *Drive: The surprising truth about what motivates us*. Riverhead Hardcover.

Ryan, R., & Deci, E. (2000). Intrinsic and extrinsic motivations: Classic definitions and new directions. *Contemporary Educational Psychology, 25*(1), 54–67. doi:10.1006/ceps.1999.1020

Schwartz, S. (2006). A theory of cultural value orientations: Explication and applications. *Comparative Sociology, 5*(2–3), 137–182. doi:10.1163/ej.9789004170346.i-466.55

Sudan, J. (2013). Gamification—Extrinsic vs. Intrinsic rewards. Playful Wingmen. http://www.slideshare.net/playfulwingmen/gamification-extrinsic-vs-intrinsic-rewards-17681228. Accessed January 3, 2015.

Thaler, R. H., & Sunstien, C. R. (2009). *Nudge: Improving decisions about health, wealth and happiness*. Penguin.

Triandis, H. C. (1977). *Interpersonal behaviour*. Monterey, CA: Brooks/Cole Publishing Company.

Trompenaars, F., & Hampden-Turner, C. (1998). *Riding the waves of culture*. New York: McGraw-Hill.

Usunier, J. C., & Lee, J. (2005). *Marketing across cultures*. Pearson Education.

Vasalou, A., et al. (2014). Problematizing cultural appropriation. In: *Proceedings of the first ACM SIGCHI Annual Symposium on Computer-Human Interaction in Play* (pp. 267–276). ACM. doi:10.1145/2658537.2658689

Wu, M. (2011). Gamification 101: The psychology of motivation—Lithium Community. *Lithium*. http://community.lithium.com/t5/Science-of-Social-blog/Gamification-101-The-Psychology-of-Motivation/ba-p/21864. Accessed November 18, 2014.

Wu, M. (2014). How to design for long-term behaviour change—Part 1. *Lithium Community*. http://community.lithium.com/t5/Science-of-Social-blog/How-to-Design-for-Long-Term-Behaviour-Change-Part-1-New-Habit/ba-p/160584. Accessed November 16, 2014.

Xu, Y. (2012). *Literature review on web application gamification and analytics*. HI: Honolulu.

Zichermann, G., & Cunningham, C. (2011). Gamification by design: Implementing game mechanics in web and mobile apps. O'Reilly Media, Inc.

Chapter 3
Gamification Analytics—Methods and Tools for Monitoring and Adapting Gamification Designs

Benjamin Heilbrunn, Philipp Herzig and Alexander Schill

Abstract Gamification analytics describe methods and tools that help to monitor the success of gamification projects, to understand a user's behaviour, and to adapt gamification designs. Even though experts agree on the importance of these activities, concrete processes and software tools have not been investigated yet. This chapter advocates and introduces gamification analytics related activities based on the findings of a study with gamification experts and illustrates them in a hypothetical gamification scenario. In the following, we identify and assess tools regarding their applicability for the presented analytical activities. This chapter helps practitioners to implement a data-driven monitoring and adaptation process within gamification projects and supports them in corresponding technology-decisions. The conclusion provides researchers with a basis for further research in the gamification analytics domain.

3.1 Introduction

The introduction of gamification can be considered successful when the desired psychological and behavioural outcomes have been achieved. Understanding requires collecting and analysing gamification related data and is a non-trivial task that should receive attention when planning a gamification project. The process of developing a gamification design entails a creative aspect and must incorporate many aspects such as the personas of involved users, the application's domain, properties of the gamified application itself, or legal constraints. These variable

B. Heilbrunn (✉) · P. Herzig
SAP SE, Potsdam, Germany
e-mail: benjamin.heilbrunn@sap.com

P. Herzig
e-mail: philipp.herzig@sap.com

A. Schill
TU Dresden, Dresden, Germany
e-mail: alexander.schill@tu-dresden.de

© Springer International Publishing Switzerland 2017
S. Stieglitz et al. (eds.), *Gamification*, Progress in IS,
DOI 10.1007/978-3-319-45557-0_3

31

parameters mean that gamification designs are not rigid artefacts, but subject to change over time. The particular reasons for changes are manifold, for example:

- The gamification design might not help to achieve the defined goals as expected;
- Certain gamification elements might not influence the behaviour of all targeted users in the intended way;
- Changes to the goal setting (e.g., due to organisational changes) might make an adaptation of the gamification design necessary;
- User engagement might slowly decrease in relevant metrics and as a result, existing gamification elements might be adjusted.

By monitoring and analysing gamification related data, gamification experts can gain valuable insights and take corresponding actions towards goal achievement. Relevant data sources comprise user behaviour data, user properties, and gamification data. User behaviour data describes user actions in the gamified application, e.g., creating a new message thread in an online community. User properties describe known properties of the end users of the gamified application, e.g., gender or geographical location. Finally, gamification data represents gamification element-related information, comprising the gamification state and user progression over time.

We define gamification analytics as the data-driven processes of monitoring and adapting gamification designs. Gamification experts have agreed that these activities are crucial to the long-term success of gamification projects (Kumar and Herger 2013). However, gamification analytics have not yet received significant attention from academics nor from a practical perspective. To address this gap, this chapter advocates for and describes activities for monitoring and adapting gamification designs. The presented concepts are mainly based on a requirements study which was conducted with 10 gamification experts from various domains and functions (Heilbrunn et al. 2014a). The remainder of this chapter is structured as follows: Sect. 3.2 presents and discusses gamification analytic related activities in gamification projects. Section 3.3 identifies and assesses tools for gamification analytics. Finally, Sect. 3.4 provides a summary and an outlook.

3.2 Activities in Gamification Analytics

This section describes and discusses analytic related activities in the context of gamification projects. The presented activities extend the gamification process model of Herzig et al. (2014). The process model consists of the following phases: (1) *Business Modelling and Requirements*, (2) *Design Workflow*, (3) *Implementation*, (4) *Monitoring and Adaptation*. To illustrate the activities, a hypothetical scenario of gamifying an IT-ticket system is used.

3.2.1 Business Modelling and Requirements

The business modelling and requirements workflows are conducted at the beginning of a gamification project. In this phase, experts analyse the context and relevant issues of the application that should be gamified. As a result of the phase *'business modelling and requirements'*, a common understanding of the business goals behind the planned introduction of gamification should be achieved. Moreover, these goals should not only be documented in textual form, but also in the form of operationalisations that unambiguously define how the achievement of business goals will be measured. Accordingly, the defined operationalisations establish the basis for continuously monitoring the success of the gamification design, which will be developed later. In the following we will use the gamification of an imaginary IT-ticket system to exemplify the presented activities. The purpose of the IT-ticket system is aimed at helping customers in IT-related issues. For this, customers can create IT-tickets. Those tickets are processed by IT service engineers who are responsible for helping the customers with their IT issues. To avoid the duplication of tickets due to common IT problems, a FAQ-site is maintained to provide solutions for frequent IT issues. Given this hypothetical scenario, Table 3.1 presents a set of three relevant business goals and their corresponding operationalisations.

3.2.2 Design Workflow

The process step *'design workflow'* builds on the results of the process step *'business modelling and requirements'*. It deals with the construction of a meaningful gamification design that addresses the earlier identified issues in an appealing way by incorporating the findings of the first phase. Prototypes may be built and play-tested for early validation.

One of the main activities in the process step *'design workflow'* is to creatively apply a set of gamification elements and mechanics that are likely to increase user engagement in the goal metrics. When envisioning gamification elements, designers

Table 3.1 Example of business goals and their operationalisations in the context of an IT-Ticket System

#	Business goal	Operationalisation
1	The number of tickets concerning problems that have well-known solutions should be low	The number of ticket responses that reference an FAQ article should be less than 5 %
2	The processing time of tickets should be low	On average the tickets should be completed within less than 6 working hours
3	Customer satisfaction with regards to processed tickets should be very high	The average customer feedback ratings on a scale between 1 and 5 should be greater than 4

often have particular intentions about how those elements should work in practice. For example, by envisioning which fraction of the users should complete a gamification element, or how much time people should spend to complete a gamification element. These intentions can be documented and thus monitored after releasing the gamification design. Deviations from these intentions are valuable insights and indicators for the fact that the gamification design does not work in the initially expected way. Consequently, adaptations might be necessary.

Assuming that IT service engineers receive points for satisfied customers with which they can advance in levels, the gamification designer could, for example, define that the final level in the gamification design should not be achieved by more than 5 % of the users. A violation of this threshold might result in an adaptation which increases the difficulty or extends the design by new levels, thus reintroducing motivation to the users who are on the formerly highest level. Another example could be that users should not reach the final level in less than one month. A violation of this threshold might as well lead to an adaptation of the gamification design.

3.2.3   Implementation

During the '*implementation*' phase, the conceptual gamification design is transformed into executable software artefacts and functionally tested. Typically, a gamification platform will be used to implement gamification related functionality. If not done earlier, the application that is being gamified has to be instrumented to provide events for user actions of relevance for gamification mechanics or gamification analytics. From the perspective of gamification analytics, these events have to comprise all information which is needed to calculate the previously defined business goal operationalisations. Additionally, the application should emit events that inform the gamification analytics solution about relevant user properties such as gender or geographical location. This data can help to optimise a gamification design for specific target groups within the end users. Table 3.2 shows a set of event definitions that can be used to measure the business goal operationalisations from Table 3.1.

Table 3.2 Necessary events for measuring business goals

Event type	Attributes	Relevant for business goals
ticket_created	ticket_id creation_timestamp	(2) Processing time
ticket_processed	ticket_id duplicates_faq closing_timestamp	(1) Fraction of FAQ duplicates (2) Processing time
ticket_rated	ticket_id rating	(3) Customer satisfaction rating

The operationalisations of business goals can be implemented in the form of formulas or queries in the history of collected application events. In the following, such formulas will be called *application KPIs* (i.e., *key performance indicators*).

Given the IT-ticket system scenario with the event definitions given in Table 3.2, experts can define the application KPIs shown in Table 3.3. For illustrative purposes, we assume that events are stored in a SQL-Database. Accordingly, calculating application KPIs is implemented by querying event tables.

3.2.4 Monitoring and Adaptation

The phase '*monitoring and adaptation workflows*' embodies the core of gamification analytic related activities. While the activities of previous phases establish prerequisites for conducting analyses, this phase eventually leverages those efforts to provide benefit to gamification experts. It comprises the activities of monitoring business goal achievement, analysing the gamification state, and adapting the gamification design in case of deviations, or changes to the goal setting.

3.2.4.1 Inspection and Exploration of Application Data

The status of the business goal achievement is measured by application KPIs which are operationalisations of business goals. Application KPIs are calculated on the basis of user behaviour events originating from the gamified application. Unfulfilled goals or negative trends within application KPIs can be starting points for a deeper investigation of user behaviours. If lower level issues, such as usability flaws can be discarded as reasons for the observed goal deviation, an adaptation of the gamification design might be necessary.

Figure 3.1 shows a hypothetical situation in the IT-ticket system scenario. One can see that for each of the business goals one application KPI is being monitored. The goals concerning (1) *ticket processing time* and (2) *customer satisfaction* are

Table 3.3 Application KPI Implementations based on events in a SQL Database

#	Application KPI query
1	**SELECT** num_faq_duplicates/total **AS** FRACTION_OF_FAQ_DUPLICATES **FROM** (**SELECT COUNT**(*) **AS** num_faq_duplicates **FROM** *ticket_processed* **WHERE** *duplicates_faq* = **true**), (**SELECT COUNT**(*) **AS** total **FROM** *ticket_processed*)
2	**SELECT AVG**(tp.*closing_timestamp* – tc.*creation_timestamp*) **AS** AVG_PROCESSING_TIME **FROM** *ticket_processed* **AS** tp **JOIN** ticket_created **AS** tc **ON** (tc.ticket_id = tp.ticket_id)
3	**SELECT AVG**(*rating*) **AS** AVG_RATING **FROM** *ticket_rated*

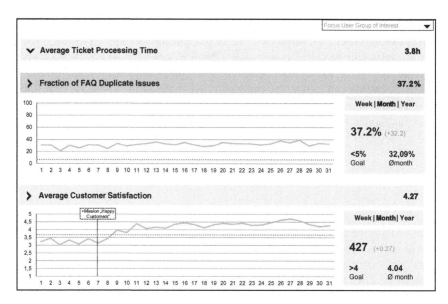

Fig. 3.1 Hypothetical application KPI setting

currently fulfilled. In particular, the development of the average customer satisfaction shows a positive trend after the gamification design was extended with a
new mission. However, business goal (3) '*FAQ duplicate issues*' shows a strong
and continuous deviation from the targeted goal value. In particular, last month's
average deviated by +27 % from the goal of a maximum of 5 %. Assuming, that
there are no other issues which hold people back from viewing the FAQ before
opening a ticket, this might be a good starting point to consider the introduction of
gamification elements that encourage users to check the FAQs before creating a
new ticket.

It is important to note that by only measuring application KPIs it is not possible
to infer causal relations between gamification design elements and the resulting
application KPI values. Any factor such as technical problems, usability flaws, or
even seasonal trends can cause changes in application KPIs. Application KPIs alone
are only indicators which can be the start for deeper investigations. With A/B
testing, gamification experts can overcome this limitation and start making
evidence-based design decisions.

3.2.4.2 Inspection and Exploration of Gamification Data

Gamification metrics embody the second important aspect to be monitored in
gamification designs. By investigating how users progress in the gamification
design, experts can validate their initial design intentions, identify issues, and gain
an understanding of how particular user groups interact with gamification elements

in the application. In the following, metrics which have been identified as relevant will be presented and discussed.

Gamification Feedback Rate

Feedback is an important element of games (Tekinbaş and Zimmerman 2004; Zichermann and Cunningham 2011; Werbach and Hunter 2012). *Gamification feedback* is any state change in the game that the user perceives as a success, e.g., by gaining points or receiving a badge. Correspondingly, the feedback rate describes the total amount of feedback per time users spent in the gamified application. Inspecting charts and statistics of the feedback rate can help experts to qualify further observations and can be a starting point for investigating surprising observations. For example, noticing that the gamified IT-ticket system has an average rate of 0.1 feedbacks per hour could be an indicator that the current gamification design lacks comprehensiveness.

Point Distributions

Inspecting the distribution of points over users can help experts to detect flaws in the balance of point amounts for gamified actions. For example, noticing that 1 % of the users own 90 % of the points might be an indicator that the point amount for gamified actions should be reconsidered.

Achievable Gamification Elements

Gamification experts can explore user progression statistics of achievable gamification elements such as badges, levels, or missions to see the overall progression of users in the gamification design. This can help to understand how attractive particular gamification elements are and to identify aspects of the gamification design where adaptations may make sense. A gamification design might, for example, require adaptation, when already 60 % of the users have reached the highest level. Assuming that gamification experts defined their design intentions, the system could also automatically inform them about violations of design intentions.

Detailed Gamification Element Statistics

An option to drill down to particular gamification elements can give experts the chance to better understand detailed aspects of user behaviour in the context of a particular gamification element.

- *User Distribution* on *Gamification Element State*: Users can have multiple states in relation to a particular gamification element. For missions, typical states, for example, comprise Mission Completed, Mission Active, and Not Assigned to Mission (Dormans 2012). Furthermore, gamification elements can have inner progress in the form of scaled intermediate goals or interval-scaled progression towards its achievement. By visualising the distribution of users in these states, gamification experts can understand how the users progress in the context of the gamification element. Experts could, for example, notice that only a few users completed a particular mission while most others are stuck in one particular sub-goal of that mission. This might be an indication that the design of the mission needs adjustment.

- *Temporal Statistics*: Experts can analyse how long users need for the completion of particular gamification elements. Relevant measures in this aspect are: *Time to Completion*, the time period between the start of user existence and gamification element completion; *Time to Assignment*, the time period between the start of user existence and its assignment to the gamification element; *Time Active*, the time period between assignment and completion of the gamification element. For example, noticing that users typically complete a mission faster than expected might be an indicator for necessary adjustments to the mission design.

- *User Characteristics*: Some gamification elements might be more attractive to particular groups of users than to others. To identify such constellations, gamification experts can explore which properties users have in common, who share the same state on a particular gamification element. Properties can be gamification properties or user properties. Gamification properties originate from the user's state in the game, e.g., owns badge A, while user properties originate from the information the application has about the user, e.g., from geographical region Europe. By revealing significant factors of user engagement in the context of a particular gamification element, experts have the chance to optimise the gamification design for their individual audience. When experts notice that a mission is significantly more often completed by European users for example, they could start investigating the reasons and adapt it to raise its attractiveness in all relevant geographical regions.

3.2.4.3 Gamification Design Adaptation

Tests with experimental and control groups (A/B tests) are a widely used method for evaluating the effects of changes in a particular context. They have also been proposed for validating gamification design ideas (Kumar and Herger 2013; Kapp 2014). With A/B testing, the effects of gamification design changes can be verified before activating them for the whole user base. Accordingly, experts can test whether a new version of the gamification design provides a better achievement of business goals.

An A/B test in the gamification domain is characterised by the size of the experimental group, affected application KPIs, the desired impact on those KPIs (increase or decrease), and the actual design changes which are subject to the experiment. After specifying the mentioned parameters and starting the experiment, a user group with the selected experiment size should start interacting with the new design. In the next step, experts can use the recorded behaviour data to analyse whether the experiment was successful. The size of the experimental group is of particular interest since it carries a trade-off between expected confidence and potential damage of the experiment. Bigger experimental groups will usually help to achieve more reliable results. However, they also embody a higher potential damage since unsuccessful changes will immediately affect a larger user base.

As an intermediate and final result of A/B tests, experts can analyse the measured effects in observed user behaviour for the experimental group as well as the control group. This helps to understand the effects and side effects of conducted changes. Together with statistical significance tests, which help to avoid misinterpretations based on sampling errors, A/B testing supports objective decision-making in the design adaptation process. As a result of keeping a new design idea, a new annotation should be created in all relevant graphical charts (see Fig. 6.1). Such change annotations in charts can help experts to keep track of historical changes and their corresponding effects. Besides changes after A/B testing, other events of relevance to user behaviour might be recorded as well. This can include major changes to the application itself or direct changes to the gamification design. The latter might be necessary in cases when A/B tests are not suitable, e.g., with small user groups or when time constraints apply.

3.2.4.4 User Groups of Interest

The behaviour of particular segments within the group of users might be of special interest for gamification experts. Therefore, experts can filter statistical overviews, such as application KPIs, gamification element statistics, or the result presentation of A/B tests using earlier defined user groups. When defining user groups, the group criteria can be known a priori, or may be discovered dynamically.

Criteria Based Definition

Criteria based user groups are determined based on a set of conditions which are evaluated against the user's properties. This approach is applicable when the exact criteria are well known before creating the user group. In the IT-ticket scenario, experts might be interested in defining user groups for each of the involved roles: customers who create tickets and service engineers who process tickets.

Cluster Analysis-Based Discovery and Definition

Cluster analysis aims at finding similar groups in a set of objects (Everitt et al. 2011). In the field of gamification, this can be applied to discover sets of users who show similar behaviour. Experts can conduct cluster analyses on relevant properties of users to discover groups which are of interest to them. This approach is applicable when the exact criteria of the user group are not known a priori. In the IT-ticket scenario, experts might be interested in discovering user groups based on their role in the system, the amount of earned points, or geographical region.

3.2.4.5 Simulation

Simulations are a common tool in the *game design* phase (Dormans 2012). In gamification design they are also considered as useful in supporting early design decisions (Rimon 2013). Gamification experts can simulate their early design ideas with existing user and behaviour data. Given that an appropriate dataset of historical user behaviour exists, a simulation can help to identify major flaws in the mechanics of a new gamification design. In the IT-ticket system scenario, experts might be interested in testing the first draft of point amounts for gamified actions. Based on the resulting point distribution across players they could then decide whether the concept is reasonable.

3.3 Tool Support for Gamification Analytics

The previous section presented gamification analytics related activities as part of the gamification process. It is evident that a holistic support of gamification analytics is complex. Therefore, sophisticated tool support is necessary to leverage the presented concepts in practice. The aspect of implementing gamification designs in software applications is well supported by gamification platforms such as *Bunchball, Badgeville*, or the *SAP Gamification Platform* (Herzig et al. 2012; Badgeville 2014; Bunchball 2014a). However, as shown in a previous survey, so far the use of specialised tools to monitor and adapt gamification designs is not common (Heilbrunn et al. 2014a). Instead, many interviewed experts have reported that they are making use of customised, narrowly focused solutions for reporting purposes. Those solutions are expensive to implement and maintain and do not address a majority of relevant requirements. To address this issue, we conducted a survey among potentially relevant tools for gamification analytics (Heilbrunn et al. 2014b). First, we considered solutions that directly advertise gamification analytics. Candidates were identified by querying internet search engines and the digital libraries of IEEE, ACM as well as Google Scholar with the terms *gamification analytics* and *gamification data analysis*. The search resulted in the identification of only two relevant tools. Thus, we decided to also consider tools from the similar game analytics domain (El-Nasr et al. 2013). The search was analogously conducted by querying IEEE, ACM, and Google Scholar with the terms *game analytics* and *game data analysis* and resulted in the identification of five relevant tools. In the following, the seven identified candidate solutions will be presented and briefly discussed with regards to their applicability in gamification projects as determined by the requirements which were identified in the preceding study.

3.3.1 Bunchball Nitro Analytics

Bunchball Nitro Analytics is part of the *Bunchball Nitro Gamification Platform*. Its assessment took place on the basis of its documentation (Bunchball 2014b). The tool offers a set of pre-defined reports and a user segmentation feature. Reports include metrics such as *number of new users*, *number of total users*, or *points awarded*. The tool can help experts to obtain a high-level understanding of user behaviour. However, from the perspective of gamification analytics activities that are discussed in this chapter, it does not provide appropriate support: The aspects of defining and monitoring application KPIs are not supported. Furthermore, the discussed gamification metrics and detailed gamification element statistics are also mostly unsupported. *Bunchball* merely provides a documented report with regards to the *Points Balance*. Since there was no sufficient evidence to assume the opposite, the activity of inspecting the point distribution is probably fulfilled. Finally, the adaptation of gamification designs, identification and persistent definition of user groups of interest, as well as simulation are also not supported by the tool.

3.3.2 Gigya Gamification Analytics

Gigya Gamification Analytics is part of the *Gigya Gamification Platform* which mainly targets gamification of online communities. It was assessed based on its documentation (Gigya 2014). The embedded analytics offer a set of predefined reports which focus on standard metrics and social metrics such as *new registered users*, *new social network connections*, or the most influential users (*key influencers*). The tool can help experts to obtain a very high-level understanding of user behaviour. However, from the perspective of gamification analytics activities that are discussed in this chapter, it does not provide appropriate support: The aspects of defining and monitoring application KPIs, gamification design adaptation processes, identification and persistent definition of user groups of interest, as well as simulation are not supported by the tool. The discussed gamification metrics are partially supported. *Gigya Gamification Analytics* supports progression reports for levels and missions. However, support for badges is missing on this level. The solution provides no mechanism for investigating how many users own a particular badge. Detailed gamification element statistics are also not supported.

3.3.3 DeltaDNA

DeltaDNA is a game analytics tool which mainly targets monetisation in Free-to-Play (F2P) games. It was assessed based on its documentation and a demo account (deltaDNA 2014). It comes with a predefined set of event types and dashboards which are specialised to relevant metrics of the F2P domain. The solution can be populated with events of arbitrary structures and retrieved events are stored in a data warehouse. There they can be queried through an integrated *Business Intelligence* tool which allows multidimensional analysis of recorded event data by executing queries in *Multidimensional Expressions* (MDX) language. The BI tool can be leveraged for defining custom KPIs or implementing gamification metrics. However, each metric needs to be defined and maintained manually which radically reduces the comfort that an automated solution could have.

The tool supports the process of A/B testing in a generic form, which requires the actual variation logic to reside in the client application. Accordingly, an adaptation of the gamification design from within the analytics solution is not possible. Experts can analyse A/B test results by comparing gamification metric values of previously defined user groups. *DeltaDNA* provides significance testing for the frequency-difference of an initially defined *conversion event*. However, measuring the impact of changes on application KPIs is not possible. In consequence, A/B testing is considered to not be supported in the expected way. Applying changes and creating corresponding change annotations are also not supported.

DeltaDNA supports the persistent definition of user groups of interest based on criteria and cluster analysis, however with major limitations. Criteria based user groups can only be defined based on *DeltaDNA*'s predefined user model and predefined metrics. Accordingly, a user's gamification metrics or application KPI values, such as an engineer's average ticket processing time, cannot be taken into account. Furthermore, the tool supports interactive 3-dimensional plots based on the set of predefined user properties and metrics which should help users to identify interesting user clusters. However, no algorithm for cluster analysis is available for automatic cluster detection. Finally, simulation is also not supported in *DeltaDNA*.

3.3.4 GameAnalytics

GameAnalytics is a game analytics tool which mainly targets monetisation in F2P games. It was assessed based on its documentation and a demo account (GameAnalytics 2014). *GameAnalytics* comes with a predefined set of event types and dashboards which are specialised to relevant metrics of the F2P domain. Custom events are supported, however they must comply with a predefined structure. In consequence, they cannot be adapted for specific use cases. The event structures presented in Table 3.2 could, for example, not be realised in GameAnalytics.

The solution comes with a query editor that can be used for the definition of custom KPIs. The query editor provides the functions *sum, mean, count* and *histogram*. GameAnalytics is therefore capable of calculating the application KPI (3) *average satisfaction rating*. However, more complex examples which require basic arithmetical operations or event correlation such as (1) *fraction of FAQ duplicates* and (2) *average processing* time cannot be implemented. Modelled application KPIs can be visualised in customisable dashboards which support charts as well as descriptive statistics.

GameAnalytics supports customised metrics that count the frequency of a particular event. The number of gamification feedbacks, as well as the progress of users in achievable gamification elements can be measured. However, since GameAnalytics cannot normalise the event count by the session length of users, the feedback rate measure is not implementable. Furthermore, the manual implementation of progress monitoring requires a high initial effort and also causes high maintenance effort when the gamification is adapted.

A/B testing can be realised partially by leveraging the *build* attribute in GameAnalytics' predefined event structure. This attribute can be used to distinguish events originating from different versions of the gamified application. Metrics of each version can then be compiled together in one chart to compare them with each other. However, creating experiments, significance testing, applying changes, or creating corresponding change annotations are not supported. The persistent definition of user groups of interest is not supported. However, similar functionality exists in some aspects, because overviews can be filtered by properties of a predefined user model. Finally, simulation is not supported in *GameAnalytics*.

3.3.5   GAMEhud

GameHud is a game analytics tool which mainly targets monetisation in F2P games. It was assessed based on its set of advertised features (GAMEhud 2014). The tool comes with a predefined set of event types and dashboards which are specialised to relevant metrics of the F2P domain. Moreover, it can be populated with events of arbitrary structures. These events can be analysed by a manual criteria-based query tool and a funnel analysis tool. Assuming that explicit events exist for each metric, the query tool can be leveraged for counting the frequency of gamification feedbacks and the number of completions of a particular achievable gamification element. The funnel tool can be used to measure the distribution of users on the state of sequential gamification elements. However, queries cannot be saved or visualised in charts that have a time dimension. Complex expressions, for example, normalising the number of feedbacks by average session length, or normalising the number of achievers by the total number of users are not supported. Finally, user groups of interest, A/B testing, and simulation are not supported by *GameHud*.

3.3.6   HoneyTracks

HoneyTracks is a game analytics tool which mainly targets monetisation in F2P games. It was assessed based on its documentation and a demo account

(HoneyTracks 2014). The tool comes with a predefined set of event types and dashboards which are specialised for relevant metrics of the F2P domain. Custom events are supported, however, they must comply with a predefined structure. In consequence, they cannot be adapted for specific use cases. The event structures presented in Table 3.2 could, for example, not be realised in *HoneyTracks*. Customised KPIs can be created and visualised in charts; however, they are limited to counting event frequency. Aggregation functions, complex expressions, or event correlation as required for the application KPI examples from Table 3.3 are not supported. *HoneyTracks* supports visual change markers in charts.

Assuming that explicit events exist for each metric, the number of gamification feedbacks as well as the progress of users in achievable gamification elements can be measured by counting the frequency of corresponding events. However, since *HoneyTracks* cannot normalise the event count by the session length of users, the feedback rate measure cannot be implemented. Furthermore, the manual implementation of progress monitoring requires high initial effort and also causes high maintenance effort when the gamification design is adapted. *HoneyTracks* partially supports A/B testing by allowing gamification experts to manually assign users to groups. These groups can then be used for direct comparison within charts. The persistent definition of user groups of interest is not supported. However, similar functionality exists in some aspects, because overviews can be filtered by properties of a predefined user model. Finally, simulation is not supported in *HoneyTracks*.

3.3.7 Upsight

From gamification analytics perspective, *Upsight*'s features are almost equivalent to the features of *HoneyTracks*. The only difference is that *Upsight* does not provide mechanisms for analysing A/B test data.

3.3.8 Assessment Result Summary

Table 3.4 provides an overview of the assessment results for the discussed tools. The assessment shows that the integrated solutions of gamification vendors (*Bunchball*, *Gigya*) provide rather simplistic analytics support. The available functionality addresses only a minority of relevant requirements for the activities that were outlined in Sect. 3.2. The activities relating to application KPI monitoring, gamification design adaptation, user groups of interest, and simulation are completely unsupported by both assessed gamification platforms. Even the category of gamification element analytics is almost completely unsupported. We conclude

Table 3.4 Tool assessment results

Requirement		Bunchball	Gigya	DeltaDNA	GameAnalytics	gameHUD	HoneyTracks	Upsight
Application KPI Monitoring	Definition of Custom Application KPIs	↓	↓	↑	↗	↓	↘	↘
	Definition of Application KPI Goal Values	↓	↓	↓	↓	↓	↓	↓
	Presentation of Application KPIs in Dashboard	↓	↓	↓	↑	↓	↗	↗
	Support for Change Markers in Charts	↓	↓	↓	↓	↓	↑	↑
	Support for KPI Goal Markers in Charts	↓	↓	↓	↓	↓	↓	↓
Gamification Element Statistics	Presentation of Gamification Feedback Rate	↓	↓	↗	↘	↘	↘	↘
	Presentation of Point Distribution over Users	↑*	↓	↑	↓	↓	↓	↓
	Overview for Statistics of Achievable Gamification Elements	↓	↘	↗	↘	↘	↘	↘
	Presentation of User Distribution on Gamification Element State	↓	↓	↓	↓	↓	↓	↓
	Presentation of Temporal Gamification Element Statistics	↓	↓	↓	↓	↓	↓	↓
	Analysis of Significant User Characteristics	↓	↓	↓	↓	↓	↓	↓
	Alerting on Violation of Design Intentions	↓	↓	↓	↓	↓	↓	↓
Gamification Design Adaptation	Experiment Result Definition	↓	↓	↘	↓	↓	↓	↓
	Experiment Result Analysis	↓	↓	↘	↘	↓	↘	↓
	Direct Design Adaptation	↓	↓	↓	↓	↓	↓	↓
User Groups of Interest	User Groups of Interest based on Criteria	↓	↓	↘	↘	↓	↘	↘
	User Groups of Interest based on Cluster Analysis	↓	↓	↘	↓	↓	↓	↓
	Filtering of Overviews by User Groups of Interest	↓	↓	↘	↘	↓	↘	↘
Simulation	Simulation based on Existing User Behaviour Data	↓	↓	↓	↓	↓	↓	↓

↓ Not supported	↘ Partially supported	↗ Mostly supported	↑ Fully Supported	* rating with low confidence

that gamification platforms currently do not leverage their potential of offering well-integrated gamification analytics. In consequence, they fall short in supporting the whole development cycle of gamification projects.

On the side of the standalone game analytics solutions (*DeltaDNA, GameAnalytics, GameHud, HoneyTracks, Upsight*) we see a diverse picture. Especially *deltaDNA* and *Upsight* provide decent support with regards to the discussed activities. However, direct support for concepts from the gamification domain and important functions such as A/B testing or simulation lack appropriate support. These game analytics tools can be leveraged to implement many aspects of the assessed requirements. However, the corresponding implementation effort, maintenance effort, and the resulting new data silo embody many disadvantages compared with the amount of support they currently provide.

3.4 Summary and Outlook

In this chapter, we introduced and advocated for the concept of gamification analytics. We described a process for gamification analytics. The presented analytic
related activities were based on the results of a study with experts who actively
work in the field of gamification. By following the presented process, gamification
professionals can plan their projects with the end in mind and ensure that project
success can be quantified.

As a second aspect of this chapter, we presented the results of a study that
assessed seven analytics tools regarding their applicability in the gamification
domain. The results showed that proficient tool support for monitoring and adapting
gamification designs is not available yet. While certain requirements can be covered
with existing tools, there is no single tool which supports a significant fraction of
the relevant requirements. However, gamification experts can still leverage the
presented results to make informed technology decisions in the context of individual projects. After technological support for the implementation of gamification
is broadly available, technology providers should start elaborating on support for
monitoring and adapting gamification designs after their implementation.
Appropriate tool support will help gamification experts to establish a feedback loop
between measured user behaviour and the design of gamified experiences without
the high cost of setting up and maintaining custom solutions.

References

Badgeville. (2014, March). Badgeville website. http://www.badgeville.com. Accessed March 19,
    2014.
Bunchball. (2014a, March). Bunchball website. http://www.bunchball.com. Accessed March 19,
    2014.
Bunchball. (2014b, May). Bunchball Nitro Analytics. http://www.bunchball.com/products/
    analytics. Accessed 27 May 2014.
deltaDNA. (2014, June). deltaDNA Wiki. https://wiki.deltadna.net. Accessed March 6, 2014.
Dormans, J. (2012). Engineering emergence: applied theory for game design. Creative Commons.
El-Nasr, M. S., Drachen, A., & Canossa, A. (2013). *Game analytics*. London: Springer.
Everitt, B. S., Landau, S., Leese, M., & Stahl, D. (2011). *Cluster analysis*. Chichester: Wiley.
GameAnalytics. (2014, June). GameAnalytics Docs. *GameAnalytics Docs*. http://support.
    gameanalytics.com. Accessed June 3, 2014.
GAMEhud. (2014, May). GAMEhud Features. *GAMEhud Features*. http://mygamehud.com/
    features. Accessed May 27, 2014.
Gigya. (2014, May). Gigya Gamification Analytics Docs. http://developers.gigya.com/010_
    Developer_Guide/80_Reports. Accessed May 30, 2014.
Heilbrunn, B., Herzig, P. & Schill, A. (2014a). Towards gamification analytics: Requirements for
    monitoring and adapting gamification designs. In 44. Jahrestagung der Gesellschaft für
    Informatik, Informatik 2014, Big Data—Komplexität meistern (pp. 333–344). Stuttgart: GI.
Heilbrunn, B., Herzig, P., & Schill, A. (2014b). Tools for gamification analytics: A survey. In
    *Proceedings of the 7th IEEE/ACM International Conference on Utility and Cloud Computing,
    UCC 2014* (pp. 603–608). Presented at the Conference on Utility and Cloud Computing, IEEE.

Herzig, P. Ameling, M., & Schill, A. (2012). A generic platform for enterprise gamification. In *Proceedings of the 2012 Joint Working IEEE/IFIP Conference on Software Architecture and European Conference on Software Architecture* (pp. 219–223). Washington, DC, USA: IEEE Computer Society.

Herzig, P., Ameling, M., Wolf, B., & Schill, A. (2014). Implementing Gamification: Requirements and Gamification Platforms. In T. Reiners & L. Wood (Eds.), *Gamification in Education and Business* (pp. 431–450). Cham: Springer.

HoneyTracks. (2014, June). HoneyTracks Docs. *HoneyTracks Docs*. https://docs.honeytracks.com. Accessed December 6, 2014.

Kapp, K. M. (2014). *The gamification of learning and instruction fieldbook*. San Francisco: Wiley.

Kumar, J. M., & Herger, M. (2013). *Gamification at work*. The Interaction Design Foundation.

Rimon, G. (2013, July 17). Website. *How to measure the ROI of gamification*. http://www.gamification.co/2013/07/17/how-to-measure-the-roi-of-gamification/. Accessed April 9, 2014.

Tekinbaş, K. S., & Zimmerman, E. (2004). *Rules of Play*. Cambridge: MIT Press.

Werbach, K., & Hunter, D. (2012). *For the win: How game thinking can revolutionize your business*. Philadelphia: Wharton Digital Press.

Zichermann, G., & Cunningham, C. (2011). *Gamification by design*. Sebastopol: O'Reilly Media.

Part II
Open Innovation, Collaboration and Gamification

Chapter 4
Customer-Oriented Strategies and Gamification—The Example of Open Customer Innovation

Susanne Robra-Bissantz and Christoph Lattemann

Abstract Companies today seek to deepen their relationships with customers. As a very demanding concept we observe collaboration with customers and the integration of customers in firm's value chain activities. Also companies increasingly bank on introducing game mechanisms in order to motivate common interactions. In this chapter we take Open Customer Innovation (OCI) as an example for customer relations. Starting with the problems that can be observed, we deduce possibly successful effects of gamification. Finally we introduce game mechanisms that can potentially save OCI from negative consequences and moreover serve as a guide for a serious approach to successful customer relationship management.

4.1 Introduction

Customers today are not only consuming products. Companies care for their customers in order to foster their loyalty. Furthermore, companies and customers tend to take on the roles of collaborating partners in market situations. A very intense form of this collaboration is integrating customers into companies' processes. So called *prosumers* or *co-workers* take on an active role—not only but often in innovation processes.

There are a broad range of platforms and concepts that companies use in order to integrate customers, particularly for the invention of potentially successful products. But what seemingly looks easy to understand and easy to implement may turn out to be a trap: customers may invent awkward products that no-one will ever buy,

S. Robra-Bissantz
Institut für Wirtschaftsinformatik, Technische Universität Braunschweig, Braunschweig, Germany
e-mail: s.robra-bissantz@tu-braunschweig.de

C. Lattemann (✉)
Information Management, Jacobs University Bremen, Bremen, Germany
e-mail: c.lattemann@jacobs-university.de

© Springer International Publishing Switzerland 2017
S. Stieglitz et al. (eds.), *Gamification*, Progress in IS,
DOI 10.1007/978-3-319-45557-0_4

they start co-working but may finish as quickly as they started. If the so called *Open Customer Innovation* (*OCI*), which we define as the *integration of customers in the company's innovation process*, is meant to really serve the company by tapping the potentials of collaboration with their consumers, it must be taken seriously and as a critical and ambiguous form of partnership with consumers. In this context, in this chapter we interchangeably use the term customer, prosumer and co-worker.

In this article we analyse the concept of OCI by using the known perspective of critical forms of Customer Integration (Robra-Bissantz and Lattemann 2005). For critical constellations and settings in OCI approaches we derive possible concepts that are applicable to gamification settings. First, we provide examples for game mechanisms that are supposed to prevent negative outcomes in OCI.

4.2 Open Innovation

4.2.1 Definition and Forms

In order to exploit the innovation potentials of different business partners, innovation management in companies has changed from opaque, closed processes to open and integrated concepts (Shipton et al. 2006). Social media has supported this change (Nambisan 2002). In Open Innovation firms collaboratively innovate with their business partners (Chesbrough 2003). These partners contribute by expressing their needs as well as suggestions for product and service ideas, which potentially lead to better fitting solutions. This prevents firm-internal innovators from the risk of thinking too much 'in-the-box' (Neyer et al. 2009).

As the start of every innovation process is of critical relevance but often fuzzy (Brun and Saetre 2008; Jörgensen et al. 2011), a broad range of Open Innovation concepts have been developed that are intended to better structure the innovation process: Idea Management Systems, Idea Competitions, Idea Toolkits, Idea Communities and Idea Markets. These approaches enable the integration of different stakeholders, provide different innovation processes and use various incentive systems (Von Hippel and Katz 2002).

One special form of Customer Integration that we focus on in the following is the integration of customers in the innovation process: Open Customer Innovation (OCI). Research has shown that OCI approaches result in better products for customers because their needs, desires and suggested outcomes are inherently included in the solution (Chesbrough 2003; Piller 2004; Robra-Bissantz and Lattemann 2005; Gassmann and Enkel 2006).

Open Innovation with customers can be classified by differentiating between the phases of the innovation process and by categorising the main goal of this kind of innovation concept. For example, some OCI concepts mainly focus on the needs of individual customers, others focus on a long-term integration of a group of customers, and another approach might be to use OCI as a pure marketing concept.

OCI in extreme forms may:

1. Serve as idea spotting, mainly as a marketing concept that leads to customers having fun and paying attention but does not require much effort from the customers (idea competition);
2. Identify customers' interests and likes, for example in surveys, in lead user concepts or crowd voting. Here smaller or bigger groups of customers are involved in little tasks like stating preferences or filling out a questionnaire (opinion mining);
3. Create new products, from idea finding until conception and testing, like co-creation concepts (Prahalad and Ramaswamy 2000; Piller and Stotko 2003) that ensure the long lasting success of the company. In this case customers should have a closer relationship with the company that involves knowing about its resources, target groups and chances (co-creation);
4. Provide new products on a regular basis, like in prosumer concepts (e.g., spreadshirt, www.spreadshirt.com). Similar to co-producer strategies (Bowers et al. 1990; Wikström 1996), in this approach customers play a vital role in the value creation of the company (co-producing).

4.2.2   Advantages and Risks of OCI

The advantages of an OCI for a company are that they get access to strategic assets and resources. Strategic assets come with the absorption of customers' unique knowledge. Provided that the right concepts are implemented, the customers themselves should know best what they want and what their needs are. They should be best in expressing their desires and potential solutions. User centred approaches such as Design Thinking or Integrative Thinking (Lattemann 2014) make intensive use of these strategic assets, by integrating the customer in the design and innovation process. Furthermore, the customer helps to bring creativity into the innovation process (Lattemann and Fritz 2014). On the resources side, customers can be used as an inexpensive human resource in terms of unpaid work time as OCI mostly relies on customers' intrinsic motivation or non-financial incentives. Still there are some other values that the customers may appreciate. For example, they might be able to buy a product invented by themselves and they might be proud about being included in innovation processes. If a product, invented by another customer, comes to market, at least the trust between customers exceeds the trust towards the company. Still the company presents itself as open and close to customers.

However, OCI also bears risks. These risks stem from two basic but inherent features. Firstly it still is 'only' a customer who is integrated in the company's innovation process. A customer may not be aware of the responsibilities he or she has concerning the final product. If in addition integrated customers are malevolent towards the company and are not loyal to other company's customers, they may disturb the entire innovation process by, for example, creating ideas with no use or value for the given customer base, ideas which do not fit with the company's product portfolio and are ill-designed. This will harm the business.

A second source of risks in OCI lies in the innovation itself. Innovation relies on creativity, knowledge, compelling ideas, and steady motivation of the innovators. Everybody, and also the customer, has fun while creating ideas or inventing a new product for the first time and even without any compensation. But doing so on a regular basis requires something that triggers motivation. Still, especially a 'somehow' (e.g., with money) motivated customer is not enough for creating innovative ideas as more often than not, he or she lacks creativity—in the long run.

Concerning the advantages and risks of OCI it can be concluded that there is certain potential that can be derived from the integration of customers into innovation processes. But this potential may easily lead to a situation where advantages cannot be exploited or, even worse, the company may suffer disadvantages. In order to identify pitfalls of OCI, research on customer integration and creativity are used to identify and potentially solve critical situations in OCI settings beforehand.

4.2.3 Perspective of Customer Integration

Customer Integration is defined as the integration of customers in the value creation process of a company (Robra-Bissantz and Lattemann 2005). Characteristics of customer integration are that the customer takes over pivotal tasks in the value creation as a cooperating and active partner of the company. He or she does this voluntarily, knowingly, and principally not for financial reasons.

The above described OCI is a special form of Customer Integration, situated in the innovation phase of value creation. Critical forms of OCI can be derived from critical forms of Customer Integration, namely by describing the characteristics of integration: the period, depth, object, and relationship of integration of the customer into the companies' processes (Robra-Bissantz and Lattemann 2005). In each of these dimensions a critical stage for certain forms of OCI can be reached that should be supported with additional activities.

- *Integration Period*: A singular, one-time event Customer Integration, like the idea competition, is hardly critical as customers act according to their own motivation. Longer lasting relationships that need repeating rounds of collaboration may become critical as they may go along with shrinking motivation on the co-worker's side over time and often imply a higher integration depth into firm's processes. In the case of longer relationships, a persisting cooperation of the customer has to be ensured by applying additional measures.
- *Integration Object*: Often a longer integration period goes along with more strategic tasks. As long as customers are involved in singular events and if the task is of operative nature, OCI is noncritical. But as soon as the customer is integrated for longer periods and therefore possesses special competences regarding for example product development, like in co-producing concepts, it

may be reasonable to consign him or her with executive tasks. In this case, OCI becomes critical as the integrated customer may not be replaced easily by internal resources anymore. A long time motivation must be guaranteed but additionally it must be ensured that he or she acts according to the company's goals, e.g., product innovations that fit the company and its culture.

- *Integration Depth*: In both above mentioned aspects, integrating the customer only in the surface of the company is less critical—e.g., in inventing a new design of a product or in working on additional non-critical features like in idea competitions. But a 'deep' integration of a co-worker into the innovation processes of whole products or completely new services, like in co-creation concepts, leads to changed characteristics of the customer's integration which may cause difficulties for the firm. This bears the risk that the customer becomes the only one in the company with competence to work on this or further innovations. Customer Integration in this case becomes '*production critical*'. In a co-production concept Customer Integration might end up in an '*output critical*' situation. This can be observed if the heart of a business model relies on a customer's work. Here not only the innovation work but also parts of the value generating processes in the new product or service depend on the customer. Especially in these cases, the customer may be perceived as a part of the larger company's structure and culture. OCI may then become critical as the co-worker has to represent the company's goals as a kind of a company ambassador. He or she must feel responsible for his or her work. In all kinds of high integration, mutual trust and loyalty are important.
- *Integration Relationship*: In OCI, single customers or a community of customers take over tasks which affect other customers, by defining products and services for them. As long as 'developers' and 'recipients' of the new product are identical entities, it is noncritical. But already in idea competitions or in opinion mining, problems may occur, because desired and expected functionalities, design or other features of the whole customer base may not be met. This might be the case if the co-working consumer is not a regular customer of the company, if he or she does not feel connected with the company and/or does not even like it because for example he or she buys from the competitor. Then chances are high that the co-worker invents products just for fun or even to damage the company. If the consumer is loyal to the company it may still be the case that he or she develops ideas that only fit his or her own preferences because he or she does not care about other customers. In all these cases of integration relationships the customer is faced with a quest for responsibility and furthermore acceptance of his or her new role that is equal to a member of the company.

All kinds of possibly critical forms of OCI—with longer integration periods, an integration in more strategic, production or output critical tasks and with a relationship, where developers do not equal the recipients—can be mastered with solutions that serve all customers as well as the companies. Customers then must be aware that OCI is a form of collaboration with the company. Collaboration means that customers must have the impression that they have the same goal as the company. They must be treated with equal rights and with respect. All activities that only seemingly position the company hierarchically above the customers must be avoided. This might already be that the company and customers have different access to common communication platforms—the company is for example able to delete customer contents deliberately. The collaboration must be voluntary and their motivation must be strengthened with certain incentives. Customers must be aware that they are needed, that the involvement is urgent and required and that they are responsible for positive and also sustainable good solutions.

4.2.4 Perspective of Creativity and Motivation

For successful Open Innovation, the co-worker must be creative and motivated in order to be able to positively contribute to the firm's success. There are two forms of motivation which are already discussed in this book: extrinsic and intrinsic. Co-worker's extrinsic motivation is based on his or her perspective as a customer and/or as a worker: the need for a new product or career concerns. Additionally, basic needs can be directed: fun, reputation, a need for social integration or financial interests. Incentives for co-workers, granted from the company, must match these needs and desires. A decreasing co-working arousal with a subsequent stop of collaboration automatically harms business success.

However, according to Raymond (1999), good collaboration starts by scratching a co-worker's personal itch. Thus, the critical point in OCI is the existence of a certain level of a co-worker's intrinsic motivation and deliberate participation at least in the initialising phase of the collaboration. Only this enables building a lasting basis for collaboration. It is also observed that intrinsic motivation of co-workers diminishes over time (Raymond 1999). A possibility to bypass this trend is the step-by-step substitution of intrinsic motivation by extrinsic motivation or even by financial benefits. However, the selection of the right incentive is highly critical. The wrong choice may be counterproductive as Wynn (2004) demonstrated. Socio-psychological studies have provided valuable insights for the transfer of intrinsic to extrinsic motivation (Frey and Osterloh 2002). For example, replacing intrinsic motivation by financial incentives shows that individuals will perform better at first. In the long run, the engagement will decrease in comparison to not financially rewarded co-workers (Frey and Osterloh 2002). Furthermore, the extrinsic motivation may displace the intrinsic motivation as soon as the co-worker has the impression of being supervised (Davis 1987). Therefore, OCI must be closely monitored with respect to the given situation and to the motivational level (Lattemann and Robra-Bissantz 2006).

Particularly for the innovation process, co-workers must be supported in being creative. According to Cross (2008), creativity and design ability are something that everyone has, to some extent, because it is embedded in our brains as a natural cognitive function. New, outstanding creative ideas must be reasonable and feasible. To be able to create new ideas customers must be supported in thinking divergently by interconnecting them with other customers (who think differently) or by making them leave their well-known ways of thinking and habits. To generate reasonable solutions, customers must be provided with or must have access to sufficient information and time (including endurance) to find well-grounded solutions (Sonnenburg 2007).

4.2.5 Consequences for Customer Characteristics

As a conclusion, summarising the perspectives above, serious OCI depends on customers that demonstrate the following characteristics:

- Knowledge about and identification with the goals, visions and culture of the company;
- Knowledge about the situation, products and processes of the company;
- Knowledge and sensitivity for all (also potential) customers, their needs, attitudes and preferences;
- Loyalty and trust concerning the company;
- Responsibility for former companies' tasks;
- Equality with employees, respectively workers;
- Deliberate participation and intrinsic motivation from the start;
- Well balanced extrinsic and intrinsic motivation and engagement for endurance in the long run;
- Net- and co-working with other customers;
- Interest in and capability for ideas beyond norms and tradition.

As we will show in the following section, gamification is able to foster those characteristics.

4.3 OCI and Gamification

4.3.1 Gamification

In recent years, gamification made a successful move into businesses. Any application, task, process or context can theoretically be gamified. According to Deterding et al. (2011) gamification means using gamification elements in a non-game context where they are usually not expected. This is in the given context the company's innovation process. The idea of combining gamification and open innovation (Hutter et al. 2011) and the integration of gamification in ideation platforms (e.g., Blohm et al. 2010) are not new.

Gamification's main goal is to increase the motivation of users by using game-like techniques (Shneiderman 2004; Flatla et al. 2011; Vassileva 2012), making people feel more involved when engaging with tasks (Pavlus 2010; Flury 2013), and improving people's innovation skills, competencies and creativity (Squire and Jenkins 2003; Von Ahn and Dabbish 2008; Xu 2012; Kapp 2012). This seems, at a first glance, that the concept of gamification is an ideal addition to OCI.

Following Zichermann and Linder (2010) and Reeves and Read (2009) gamification consists of certain ingredients of play that are meant to be implemented. Playing heuristics like challenge or curiosity (Malone 1982) are difficult to implement on an operative level whereas typical rules of a game are hardly generalizable. More useful are the desired outcomes of games and that games are structured by rules and a competitive process towards a goal (Deterding et al. 2011). Therefore various authors have identified gamification as a technique of applying game mechanisms to drive users to perform a desired action to reach a certain goal. Game design has to accumulate these game mechanisms that include 'a number of patterns, rules, feedback loops and governance mechanisms that are motivational, and create user engagement and loyalty' (Vassileva 2012, p. 8) in order to guide the behaviour of users (Xu 2012). Examples of well-known game mechanics are a background story, rewarding badges, game levels, points and challenges (Xu 2012).

4.3.2 Effects of Gamification

In order to explore its effects we will analyse gamification from a theoretical perspective. Research has shown that gamification leads to mental states like self-efficacy, flow (Cyskcentsmihaly 1990; Mainemelis and Ronson 2006), positive and negative emotions (Russ and Schafer 2006), a feeling of group-membership, and equality among the players (Sutton-Smith 1997). These mental states may provoke the intended behaviours (Cronk 2012). In our case the desired behaviours can be derived and summarised from the promising customers' characteristics:

- Customers should become acquainted with the company and learn about it and its goals in order to master the knowledge they need for innovation processes;
- Customers should act as a part of the company and equal to its members, share its values, be responsible and loyal towards it;
- Customers should perform their activities with creativity and motivation, cooperate with other co-workers, think divergently and unlearn.

Research has shown that most of these aspects can be fulfilled by gamification in general.

Divergent Thinking and Creativity:

Playing supports divergent thinking (e.g., Lieberman 1977; Seja and Russ 1999). It is assumed that the idea of playing is the opposite of studying or everyday life, and the outcome is interacting in a completely new business ecosystem while having fun (Simões et al. 2013). This leads to free associations and floating thoughts (Dansky and Silverman 1973, 1975) as well as to the ability to give up well-known associations (Dansky 1980). Especially the background story (as a game mechanism) and the progressing process of a game steadily confront the player with new situations. The player escapes from normal live, has to become experiential, and go beyond the limits of his or her routines and knowledge (e.g., Reeves and Read 2009).

Divergent thinking leads to creativity. Additionally, many other psychological effects of gamification lead to more and better new ideas. These include emotions (Russ 2004), self-efficacy (Bandura 1977) and group affiliation (Amabile 1988). All of that leads to new perspectives but also solutions and solving processes that the player never tried out before: a good basis for more creativity (Runco 1991).

Learning and Unlearning:

Today research agrees upon the fact that contextual embeddedness, group affiliation, as well as motivation that might be found in gaming, lead to successful learning (see last two chapters of this book). 'Unlearning', in contrast to 'forgetting', is—like learning—a result of planful action. It changes intentions, behaviours, and routines (Akgün et al. 2006; Tsang and Zahra 2008). Playing leads to unlearning via the experiments that the player starts because he or she is steadily faced with new situations. Furthermore the described divergent thinking is also able to face the obstacles in leaving good old routines (Mainemelis and Ronson 2006).

Group Affiliation, Loyalty and Equality:

If players come together, maybe even from inside and outside the company (workers and co-workers), chances are high that at the beginning of a game they agree on a common goal. Together they are keen on reaching this goal with the same set of rules and in managing their common progress (Simões et al. 2013). This leads to a feeling of group affiliation and loyalty that reaches from customers to company members and among the platform provider and the customer (Vassileva 2012). Additionally, the feeling of acting opposite from real life (Simões et al. 2013) leads to equality between all players as a foundation.

Motivation and Responsibility:

Self-efficacy and optimal challenge in a so called flow-experience (Cyskcentsmihaly 1990), together with group affiliation (as a basic motive) foster sustainable motivation on a high level (Maslow 1968; Baumeister and Leary 1995). Additionally, short motivation in gamified environments is prevented by guaranteeing that players enjoy the activity (Shneiderman 2004; Flatla et al. 2011; Vassileva 2012). Together with experiences of competence and autonomy (Vassileva 2012) as well as emotions (Okan 2003) that occur during play, players feel responsible for their outcomes. Motivation and responsibility therefore especially stem from competition mechanics like points, levels etc.

4.3.3 Game Mechanisms for OCI

Meaningful gamification (Nicholson 2015) puts the user in the centre of the design of applications in order to reach certain goals. Here, game mechanisms are applied for OCI in order to exploit its advantages, but still cope with its disadvantages. Single but prominent game mechanisms that shall be assigned to the aims concerning potentially successful OCI are taken from Björk and Holopainen (2005): the game set-up in general, the background story, levels, points, scores, choices, communities, goals, achievements, progression, badges, rewards, feedback, quests and problem solving.

To make the customers familiar and acquainted with the company, a background story might be developed and presented to the customers. Customers will be able to learn about the company and its goals in order to collect the knowledge they need for innovation processes. Quests and problem solving tasks about the company's history or vision foster competencies and provoke customers' understanding.

This is the first step for the customer that leads to feeling part of and responsible for the company and all its customers and also equal to its members. Additionally, a game set up that combines players from inside and outside the company leads to mutual understanding. Achievements and goals lead to a common path. In choices that have to be made, all players may formulate their own common goals and decisions. Communication and cooperation in communities or teams from partners both in- and outside the company lead to a feeling of belonging together and a background story, for example with different roles, makes customers feel equal to partners in the company.

All kinds of competition, like points, levels, scores etc., that are part of games stabilise motivation. Positive motivation results from incentives, success and respect—all enabled by visible marks, like badges, rewards or feedback. Progressing elements, like dices or cards may lead players through often unforeseeable situations. This, together with the background story and different roles that distract from the real world, may lead to motivation, divergent thinking and creativity.

4.4 Conclusion

With this article we chose a very demanding perspective of customer relationships and common innovation processes: OCI. We have shown that OCI contains a couple of traps: the customer might not be acquainted and related enough to the company to feel responsible for its success. Or the customer might lack motivation and creativity to innovate. However, in this chapter we pointed out that the use of gaming in general and the application of certain game mechanisms enable a more successful OCI.

The following chapters of this book build on the idea of OCI and gamification. Firstly, they make clear that the chances and risks that were shown for OCI also apply for different customer relations or customer integration processes, as well as for innovation processes in general. Secondly, to a certain extent they are able to prove some aspects of our proposition: to use gamification in order to prevent risks of sophisticated customer related strategies.

References

Akgün, A. E., Lynn, G. S., & Yılmaz, C. (2006). Learning process in new product development teams and effects on product success: A socio-cognitive perspective. *Industrial Marketing Management, 35*(2), 210–224.

Amabile, T. M. (1988). A model of creativity and innovation in organizations. *Research in Organizational Behavior, 10*(1), 123–167.

Bandura, A. (1977). Self-efficacy: Toward a unifying theory of behavioral change. *Psychological Review, 84*(2), 191.

Baumeister, R. F., & Leary, M. R. (1995). The need to belong: Desire for interpersonal attachments as a fundamental human motivation. *Psychological Bulletin, 117*(3), 497.

Björk, S., & Holopainen, J. (2005). *Patterns in game design.* Hingham, Massachusetts: Charles River Media Inc.

Blohm, I., Bretschneider, U., Leimeister, J. M., & Krcmar, H. (2010). Does collaboration among participants lead to better ideas in IT-based idea competitions? An empirical investigation. *International Journal of Networking and Virtual Organisations, 9*(2), 106–122.

Bowers, K. S., Regeher, G., Balthazard, C., & Parker, K. (1990). Intuition in the context of discovery. *Cognitive Psychology, 22*(1), 72–110.

Brun, E., & Saetre, A. S. (2008). Ambiguity reduction in new product development projects. *International Journal of Innovation Management, 12*, 573–596.

Chesbrough, H. W. (2003). The era of open innovation. *MIT Sloan Management Review, 44*, 35–42.

Cronk, R. (2012). Using gamification to increase student engagement and participation in class discussion. In *TEEM'15 Proceedings of the 3rd International Conference on Technological Ecosystems for Enhancing Multiculturality* (pp. 45–250).

Cross, N. (2008). *Engineering design methods: Strategies for product design.* New Jersey: Wiley.

Cyskcentsmihaly, M. (1990). *Flow: The psychology of optimal experience.* New York: Harper and Row.

Dansky, J. L. (1980). Make-believe: A mediator of the relationship between play and associative fluency. *Child Development,* 576–579.

Dansky, J. L., & Silverman, I. W. (1973). Effects of play on associative fluency in preschool-aged children. *Developmental Psychology, 9*(1), 38.

Dansky, J. L., & Silverman, I. W. (1975). Play: A general facilitator of associative fluency. *Developmental Psychology, 11*(1), 104.

Davis, S. (1987). *Future perfect, reading.* MA: Addison-Wesley.

Deterding S., Dixon, D., Khaled, R., & Nacke, L. (2011). From game design elements to gamefulness: Defining "gamification". In *Proceedings of the 15th International Academic MindTrek Conference: Envisioning Future Media Environments* (pp. 9–15).

Flatla, D. R., Gutwin, C., Nacke, L. E., Bateman, S., & Mandryk, R. L. (2011). Calibration games: Making calibration tasks enjoyable by adding motivating game elements. In *UIST'11—Proceedings of the 24th Annual ACM Symposium on User Interface Software and Technology* (pp. 403–412).

Flury, B. (2013). *A first course in multivariate statistics*. New York: Springer Science & Business Media.

Frey, B. S., & Osterloh, M. (2002). *Successful management by motivation. Balancing intrinsic and extrinsic incentives*. Berlin: Springer.

Gassmann, O., & Enkel, E. (2006). Open innovation. *ZfO Wissen, 3*, 132–138.

Hutter, K., Hautz, J., Fuller, J., Mueller, J., & Matzler, K. (2011). Communitition: The tension between competition and collaboration in community-based design contests. *Creativity and Innovation Management, 20*(1), 3–21.

Jörgensen, J. H., Bergenholtz, C., Goduscheit, R. C., & Rasmussen, E. S. (2011). Managing inter-firm collaboration in the fuzzy front-end: Structure as a two-edge sword. *International Journal of Innovation Management, 15*, 145–163.

Kapp, K. M. (2012). *The gamification of learning and instruction: Game-based methods and strategies for training and education*. San Francisco: Wiley.

Khaddage, F., & Lattemann, C. (2014). Mobile gamification in education—Engage, educate and entertain. In *Gamified Mobile Apps, SITE Conference 2014*.

Lattemann, C. (2014). On the convergence of corporate governance practices in emerging markets. *International Journal of Emerging Markets, 9*(2), 316–332.

Lattemann, C., & Fritz, K. (2014). Learning integrative thinking. *Society for Information Technology & Teacher Education International Conference, 2014*(1), 1857–1864.

Lattemann, C., & Robra-Bissantz, S. (2006). Customer integration–social and technology based concepts for a customer governance. *Frontiers of e-Business Research*, 193–205.

Lieberman, J. N. (1977). *Playfullness*. New York: Academic Press.

Mainemelis, B., & Ronson, S. (2006). Ideas are born in fields of play: Toward a theory of play and creativity in organizational settings. *Research in Organizational Behavior, 27*, 81–131.

Malone, T. W. (1982). Heuristics for designing enjoyable user interfaces: Lessons from computer game. In *Human Factors in Computing Systems*.

Maslow, A. H. (1968). *Toward a psychology of being*. New York: Lushena Books.

Nambisan, S. (2002). Designing virtual customer environments for new product development: Toward a theory. *Acad Manage Rev, 27*, 392–413.

Neyer, A.-K., Bullinger, A. C., & Moeslein, K. M. (2009). Integrating inside and outside innovators: A sociotechnical systems perspective. *R&D Management, 39*, 410–419.

Nicholson, S. (2015). A recipe for meaningful gamification. In T. Reiners & L. Wood (Eds.), *Gamification of education and business* (pp. 1–20). New York: Springer.

Okan, Z. (2003). Edutainment: Is learning at risk? *British Journal of Educational Technology, 34*(3), 255–264.

Pavlus, J. (2010). The game of life. *Scientific American, 303*, 43–44.

Piller, F. T.(2004). *Innovation and value co-creation* (Habilitation dissertation). University of Technology Munich.

Piller, F. T., & Stotko, C. M. (2003). *Mass customization und kundenintegration*. Düsseldorf.

Prahalad, C. K., & Ramaswamy, V. (2000). Co-opting customer competence. *Harvard Business Review, 78*, 79–87.

Raymond, E. S. (1999). The cathedral and the bazaar. Available from http://www.unterstein.net/su/docs/CathBaz.pdf. April 07, 2016.

Reeves, B., & Read, J. L. (2009). Total engagement. *Using Games and Virtual Worlds to Change the Way People Work and Businesses Compete*, 132–133.

Robra-Bissantz, S., & Lattemann, C. (2005). Customer integration und customer governance—Neue Konzepte für die Anbieter-Kunden-Beziehung im B2C-E-Business. In *Presented at the GeNeMe* (pp. 25–38). Dresden.

Runco, M. A. (1991). *Divergent thinking*. Michigan: Ablex Publishing.

Russ, S. W. (2004). *Play in child development and psychotherapy: Toward empirical practice*. New Jersey: Lawrence Erlbaum.

Russ, S. W., & Schafer, E. D. (2006). Affect in fantasy play, emotion in memories, and divergent thinking. *Creativity Research Journal, 18*(3), 347–354.

Seja, A. L., & Russ, S. W. (1999). Children's fantasy play and emotional understanding. *Journal of Clincal Child Psychology, 28*(2), 269–277.

Shipton, H., West, M. A., Dawson, J., Birdi, K., & Malcolm, P. (2006). HRM as a predictor of innovation. *Human Resource Management Journal, 16*(1), 3–27.

Shneiderman, B. (2004). Designing for fun: How can we design user interfaces to be more fun? *Interactions, 11*(5), 48–50.

Simões, J., Redondo, R. D. A., & Vilas, A. F. N. (2013). A social gamification framework for a K-6 learning platform. *Computers in Human Behavior, 29*(2), 345–353.

Sonnenburg, S. (2007). *Kooperative Kreativität: Theoretische Basisentwürfe und organisationale Erfolgsfaktoren.* Berlin: Springer.

Squire, K., & Jenkins, H. (2003). Harnessing the power of games in education. *Insight, 3*(1), 5–33.

Sutton-Smith, B. (1997). *The ambiguity of play.* Cambridge Massachusetts: Harvard University Press.

Thomas J. C., & Schneider M. L. (Eds.) (1984). *Human factors in computer systems.* Norwood: Ablex Publishing Corporation.

Tsang, E. W. K., & Zahra, S. A. (2008). Organizational unlearning. *Human Relations, 61*(10), 1435–1462.

Vassileva, J. (2012). Motivating participation in social computing applications: A user modeling perspective. *User Modeling and User-Adapted Interaction, 22*(1–2), 177–201.

Von Ahn, L., & Dabbish, L. (2008). Designing games with a purpose. *Communications of the ACM, 51*(8), 58–67.

Von Hippel, E., & Katz, R. (2002). Shifting innovation to users via toolkits. *Management Science, 48,* 821–833.

Wikström, S. (1996). The customer as co-producer. *European Journal of Marketing, 30*(4), 6–19.

Wynn, D. E. (2004). Organizational structure of open source projects: A life cycle approach. In *Proceedings of Southern Association of Information Systems* (pp. 285–299).

Xu, Y. (2012). *Literature review on web application gamification and analytics* (CSDL Technical Report 11-05). Available from http://citeseerx.ist.psu.edu/viewdoc/download?doi=10.1.1.462.5228&rep=rep1&type=pdf. April 05, 2016.

Zichermann, G., & Linder, J. (2010). *Game-based marketing: inspire customer loyalty through rewards, challenges, and contests.* New Jersey: Wiley.

Chapter 5
Obstacles and Challenges in the Use of Gamification for Virtual Idea Communities

Christian Scheiner, Philipp Haas, Ulrich Bretschneider, Ivo Blohm and Jan Marco Leimeister

Abstract Virtual idea communities (VIC) are a relatively new phenomenon in business. These communities, in which distributed groups of individual customers focus on voluntarily sharing and elaborating innovation ideas, are used by firms to integrate customers into the ideation for new product development rooted in Chesbrough's (2003) open innovation paradigm. Developers and decision makers realised especially within the last decade that games or game-like appeals could serve as appropriate gamifications to attract people to participate in VICs. Therefore, gamification gained momentum and has been widely implemented into VICs. The use of gamification does, however, not lead to the intended positive outcomes per se. Because of that, obstacles and challenges in the use of gamification have to be considered, but these have often been neglected in practice. Therefore, the goal of this chapter is to address this topic and to describe major obstacles and challenges in the use of gamification in VICs.

C. Scheiner
University of Lübeck, Lübeck, Germany
e-mail: christian.scheiner@uni-luebeck.de

P. Haas · I. Blohm · J.M. Leimeister
University of St. Gallen, St. Gallen, Switzerland
e-mail: philipp.haas@unisg.ch

I. Blohm
e-mail: ivo.blohm@unisg.ch

J.M. Leimeister
e-mail: leimeister@uni-kassel.de

U. Bretschneider (✉) · J.M. Leimeister
University of Kassel, Kassel, Germany
e-mail: bretschneider@uni-kassel.de

© Springer International Publishing Switzerland 2017
S. Stieglitz et al. (eds.), *Gamification*, Progress in IS,
DOI 10.1007/978-3-319-45557-0_5

65

5.1 Introduction

Virtual idea communities (VIC) are a relatively new phenomenon in business. These communities, in which distributed groups of individual customers focus on voluntarily sharing and elaborating innovation ideas, are used by firms to integrate customers into the ideation for new product development rooted in Chesbrough's open innovation paradigm (Chesbrough 2003) or according to the more general crowdsourcing principle (Chesbrough 2003; Afuah and Tucci 2012). Based on this paradigm, firms transcend their boundaries in order to engage other resources in developing ideas for innovations (Chesbrough 2003). In this context, customers are seen as a key resource as they often have high product expertise as well as experiences and creativity potential gained from regular product usage (Henle 1962; Amabile 1979). Many well-known companies, including DELL ('Ideastorm' VIC), Starbucks, Google, SAP, Intel, and BMW, have established VICs (Di Gangi and Wasko 2009).

Firms organise VICs from initial community building to continuous community management. This allows them to constantly control the community, from moderation of the ideation to non-restrictive use of its idea outcome. In contrast to that, already known online user innovation communities, such as open source communities, Wikipedia, or online communities of basketball enthusiasts who share ideas for improving the design or other features of sport shoes (Füller et al. 2007), are run completely by and for users, which makes it difficult for firms to harness the outcome of the communities for new product development.

By shifting customer ideation onto the Internet, firms profit from organisational benefits. First, inviting customers into VICs is less complex than organising face-to-face workshops such as focus groups or lead user workshops. Once a VIC is established, firms can constantly get back to the customer knowledge base. Furthermore, VIC's underlying IT-based idea management systems help firms to evaluate and select the most promising customer ideas. Second, VICs can help firms attain access to a much broader customer base or a customers' knowledge base, respectively (Leimeister et al. 2009). This considerably increases the likelihood of identifying a number of promising ideas for product development.

In order to achieve these benefits, firms have to be aware of the reasons and motives why people participate in VICs and have to address these motives by creating a positive and adequate experience. Developers and decision makers realised especially within the last decade that games or a game-like appeal could serve as appropriate gamifications to attract people to VICs. Gamification therefore gained momentum and has been widely implemented into VICs. However, the use of gamification does not per se lead to this intended positive outcome. Obstacles and challenges in the use of gamification have to be considered, however these have often been neglected in practice. Therefore, the goal of this chapter is to address this topic and to describe three major obstacles and challenges in the use of gamification in VICs.

The chapter is structured as follows: first, a literature review on the motivation for participation in VICs is given in Sect. 5.1. Next, gamification and its design elements are described in Sect. 5.2 before the obstacles and challenges of gamification in VICs are highlighted in Sect. 5.3. Section 5.4 presents the conclusion and possibilities for future research.

5.2 Motivation for Participation in VICs

There is evidence that customers participating in VICs have fun developing ideas (Jokisch 2007; Motzek 2007; Antikainen et al. 2010). By doing so, customers are able to satisfy their creative urge and product-related curiosity or they simply find developing ideas to be intellectually stimulating. This is discussed as the fun-motive.

A second motive is *altruism*. Customers who are motivated by altruism for example seek to help the firm enhance existing products or develop new ones without expecting any reward (Jeppesen and Frederiksen 2006; Schattke et al. 2012). For instance, Jokisch looked at motivations of customers who contributed to the BMW VIC. He found that most participants contributed because they simply wanted to help BMW (Jokisch 2007). In other words, some customers have highly altruistic attitudes towards firms.

Third, the *product innovation and enhancement-motive* is another motive. Some customers feel that by participating in VICs they can influence the firm to incorporate new product features into existing products or even develop completely new products that they find highly valuable in their own context. Their participation thus arises from their individual needs (Jokisch 2007; Motzek 2007; Antikainen et al. 2010). Further, some customers hope to accentuate the necessity of improving the functionality or a defect of the underlying product (Antikainen et al. 2010).

A fourth motivation is that customers may consider participating in virtual communities as an effective way to demonstrate their capabilities and skills shown through their contributions (Jeppesen and Frederiksen 2006; Motzek 2007). Their achievements in VICs can be used to demonstrate competence to the firm or other participants. Thus, participating can be a good channel for self-advertisement; hence, this motive is called *capability signalling-motive* or *self-marketing-motive* (Bretschneider et al. 2015).

A fifth motive is the *recognition-motive*. As Jokisch discovered, customers engage in VICs because they hope to receive positive reactions to their submitted ideas displayed on the VIC's Internet platform (Jeppesen and Frederiksen 2006; Jokisch 2007; Schattke et al. 2012). They expect positive reactions from other participants as well as from the firm. In psychological theory, recognition is derived from an individual's desire for fame and esteem (Maslow 1987; Holmström 1999). Positive recognition, for example for a certain piece of work, is described as self-reinforcing, as positive feedback enhances the motivation for expending additional effort in this or future work. This pattern is in line with VICs. Idea submitters feel proud when other customers or firms acknowledge their ideas openly within the community, and they perceive this recognition as an additional incentive for creating new ideas or elaborating existing ideas.

The next motive is the *learning-motive*. Very often customers engage in a firm's VIC to gain knowledge from the participants in the VIC (Jokisch 2007; Antikainen et al. 2010). Such customer involvement enhances customers' knowledge about the product, as well as about the underlying technologies. This, in turn, enables them to use the product in a much more comprehensive manner, thereby increasing the potential benefit of product usage (Nambisan 2002).

A further motive is called *need-motive*. Customers feel that by participating in VICs they can lobby and influence the firm to incorporate certain product features that are highly valuable in the customers' own context (Bretschneider et al. 2015). This has often been evidenced in the enterprise software product market where customers from a particular industry actively contribute to product development efforts in order to ensure that their specific needs are met by a new product (Hoch et al. 1999).

Finally, the *contact to peers-motive* is linked with getting in contact with other customers in order to make new friends or to interact with others in the virtual environment of a VIC (Bretschneider et al. 2015).

5.3 Gamification

Beyond a doubt, VICs are suitable tools for engaging customers in the ideation process, as suggested in many studies (Henle 1962; Chesbrough 2003; Afuah and Tucci 2012). As shown above, customers are encouraged by stimulating manifold intrinsic motivational factors. To do so, VICs are enriched with game design elements in order to positively influence customers' motivation and behaviour (Deterding et al. 2011; Petkov et al. 2011; Huotari and Hamari 2012). This follows the thought that games have high potential to foster motivation and creativity (Scheiner and Witt 2013). This application of game elements in a non-entertaining context is called *gamification* (Deterding et al. 2011). Of course, the aim of designing information systems to be more intrinsically encouraging is not new, but started with the beginning of personal computers. Approaches range from the design of user interfaces (Malone 1981; Carroll 1982; Carroll and Thomas 1982) to the implementation of hedonic elements (Hassenzahl 2004) and their motivational effects (Zhang 2008). Playfulness evolved as aspired user experience (Deterding et al. 2011). Central is the vanishing differentiation between the hedonic and utilitarian purpose of the information system (Dahan and Hauser 2002). Examples for such hybrid information systems in the context of VICs can be found in several studies (e.g., Franke and Piller 2004; Piller and Walcher 2006; Witt et al. 2012; Haas et al. 2013).

Table 5.1 Overview of game design elements

Game design element	*Explanation* (Scheiner and Witt 2013)
Game points	Game points are assigned automatically for the achievement of pre-defined objectives (e.g., solving a task, finishing a mission) (Hacker and Von Ahn 2009). In VICs, game points represent direct feedback for a user's performance relative to that of other participants. In VICs, game points are assigned for instance for submitting, commenting, or rating an idea. As all users receive the same number of points for the same tasks, game points are the starting point for competitive behaviour as participants are motivated to enhance their activities within the VIC
Social points	Social points are assigned by other users (e.g., community rating (Leimeister et al. 2009). In VICs, this represents direct qualitative feedback for a user's performance, such as the quality of an idea or a comment. In VICs, this can be realised for example by a simple thumbs up/down button (as seen on *YouTube*) or scales (like the five stars rating scale on *Amazon*). Social points both foster the sense of social belonging and serve as a competitive anchor, which are important conditions for an effective VIC
Redeemable points	Redeemable points represent an in-game currency, which can be spent to purchase virtual or real goods (Hamari and Lehdonvirta 2010). Thus, it enables an economic system allowing users a certain degree of autonomy for individual development and differentiation. In VICs, redeemable points can be implemented by applying market-based rating mechanisms to rate ideas (e.g., participants can make weighted decisions by assigning different amounts of points to different ideas) or to incentivise the participants (e.g., by exchanging the points for physical rewards)
Levels	Users can rise to new levels by achieving certain objectives (e.g., exceed certain points). Levels indicate a user's past performance and thus enable inter-user comparisons. Thus, levels increase the competitive character of a game. In VICs, levels can either be designed as sections, where a game is divided into smaller subtasks while the level of difficulty remains the same (Byrne 2005), or as stages, where the level of difficulty increases continuously (McGuire and Jenkins 2008). The user experiences a steadily growing optimal challenge. A typical application of levels in VICs is the implementation of user ranks
Leaderboards and high scores	Leaderboards and highscores enable immediate comparisons of users' past performances. Thus, in VICs, they are highly competitive game design elements and increase the visibility of users' performances (Von Ahn and Dabbish 2008; Reeves and Read 2009). The individual ranking within a group of peers represents a strong motivator for human behaviour (Frank 1985) and motivates the participants of a VIC to increase their activities
Exchange	Users exchange with each other due to competitive (e.g., mutual moves) or collaborative reasons (trade, support, donation) (Blau 1964). In VICs, the exchange between participants represents a core characteristic, as the collaborative development of ideas is the central objective of VICs. Through exchange, users actively partake in a social group (Sun et al. 2006). Thus, exchange satisfies the need for social belonging. In VICs, exchange is enabled by a private messaging system, commentary functions, activity streams, or forums

(continued)

Table 5.1 (continued)

Game design element	*Explanation* (Scheiner and Witt 2013)
Stories	In VICs, stories can be integrated statically or dynamically. Initial idea descriptions or background stories are examples of static stories and provide a narrative, imaginary frame and basic structure. They create a virtual world where users act or enhance the desire to participate. They link information, give meaning to the game, and help to focus on the point (Mallon and Webb 2000; Salen and Zimmerman 2004). Dynamic stories, for example continuing the idea description in a narrative way, enable interactive action where the user becomes the narrator. They allow for insights into the user's opinions and cognitive structures (Buckler and Zien 1996; Bruner 2009)
Virtual identity	Avatars are idealised self-images, which compensate for real deficits (Bessière et al. 2007). An avatar increases one's self-esteem and confidence and helps to overcome for instance hierarchy levels (McKenna and Bargh 2000). This is important in VICs, as overcoming hierarchies and silo thinking is a key success factor of VICs. Therefore, VICs often enable participants to create anonymous nicknames. In VICs, these enable individuality and differentiation between participants and support the formation of new hierarchies within the game (Jakobsson 2002)
Collecting	The collecting of rare items (e.g., badges for submitting the first/fifth/tenth idea, making 20 comments, or rating 50 ideas) works due to the desire to complete a set (Thompson et al. 2007). Collecting represents an additional opportunity to achieve social recognition and supports the competitive character of a VIC, as collected items demonstrate the social status of a user (Danet and Katriel 1989; Long and Schiffman 1997)

5.4 Game Design Elements

Game design elements are the building blocks of the gamified service bundles (Blohm and Leimeister 2013). These game design elements serve as triggers to encourage users to show a certain behaviour and to reach a defined goal (Fullerton et al. 2004; Witt et al. 2012). By forming the game, game design elements are able to foster motivation for participation, stabilise users' engagement, and strengthen their creativity (Scheiner and Witt 2013). Game design elements can be identified with different degrees of abstraction. Deterding et al. (2011) differentiated between five levels: (1) interface design patterns (Crumlish and Malone 2009); (2) game design patterns (Bjork and Holopainen 2004) or game mechanics (Taylor 2009); (3) design principles (Isbister and Schaffer 2008); (4) conceptual models (Calvillo-Gámez et al. 2010; Fullerton 2014); (5) game design methods and processes (Belman and Flanagan 2010). A comprehensive overview of the most common game design elements is presented by Scheiner and Witt 2013. This systemisation of game design elements is applied in certain studies (Witt et al. 2012; Haas et al. 2013). Scheiner and Witt (2013) differentiated between nine game design elements, which are explained and discussed in the context of VICs in Table 5.1.

The game design elements are neither new nor is their application in a professional context. According to Blohm and Leimeister (2013), the innovativeness of gamification lies in the bundling of these game design elements into 'comprehensive, IT-based and increasingly ubiquitous enhancing services', which not only provides intrinsic motivation and benefits on its own, but also affects the usage experience by offering cognitive, emotional, and social elements (Lee and Hammer 2011). Thus, the application of game design elements in the context of VICs aims at developing more and better ideas, overcoming hierarchies and silo thinking, and promoting an innovation-friendly corporate environment.

5.5   Obstacles and Challenges in the Gamification of VICs

Given the knowledge base stemming from research concerning motives for participation and gamification, gamification illustrates a promising tool to evoke positive effects among participants in VICs and to create a more enjoyable experience for participants. The application of gamification is however not easily accomplished and definitely not without obstacles and challenges. Previous endeavours and scientific research have mainly neglected this side and solely proclaimed its potential benefits and values instead. Yet, gamification can unfold its potential only under such circumstances where obstacles and challenges are addressed adequately. There are three major sources from which obstacles and challenges can arise.

The first challenge concerns the misuse of gamification by developers and decision makers. Gamification is not a standalone solution but describes the application of game design elements in a specific artefact. Developers and decision makers have to be aware that this artefact has to be constructed in such a manner that the use of game design elements contributes to the creation of an enjoyable experience (Füller 2006; Scheiner 2015). Hence, functionalities of the artefact have to be interwoven with the chosen game design elements. Game design elements are otherwise not perceived as an integral part but as disturbing or distracting elements. Game design elements also have to be aligned with the overall objective of the VIC to guide the activities of participants toward that objective (Scheiner and Witt 2013). Simultaneously, the motive structure of participants has to be kept in mind in order to offer a working incentive scheme (Blohm and Leimeister 2013). In practice however, it can be observed regularly that decision makers believe that game design elements unfold their motivational effect automatically regardless of the motive structure of participants. Yet, there is a huge difference between game design elements with a social character and those without. Social points and exchange for instance can contribute to an overall social appeal of the artefact, where the motive of recognition and being in contact with others can be fostered. In all these cases, the misuse can reduce or even diminish the potential of gamification completely. At the same time, misuse can also mean that gamification is too effective and becomes an end in itself or a burden for participants. Werbach and Hunter (2012) pointed to the misuse of gamification where it is too effective and becomes a burden for participants. They described the case of Disneyland hotels in Anaheim, where the performance of laundry workers was measured with a gamified system and was displayed in the form of leaderboards. The introduction and implementation of this system negatively influenced the working climate by creating an atmosphere of fear. Bogost argued for this reason in his blog provocatively in (2011) that gamification resembles a 'perversion of games' and suggested the term 'exploitationware'. To avoid these negative consequences, Schell (2008) advocated that developers and decision makers should be aware of the danger of gamification and their respon-sibility in order to ensure ethical use. When rewards are an end in itself, reaching a new level, improving one's own position in a leaderboard, or collecting a new badge can become so important that participants direct their focus on activities solely towards these rewards, while the underlying objective of the VIC is pushed into the background.

The second challenge is closely linked to the previous challenge. If rewards become too important, participants could start to game the system. In cases where self-marketing is a main trigger for participation, participants could especially try to gain an unfair advantage by manipulating the system. A common approach to play a VIC illustrates the formation of cartels. Participants build groups and show a concerted behaviour in order to promote their goals and ideas. This is expressed for instance by awarding each other points, by writing positive comments to each other, or by trying to negatively influence the public evaluation of competing ideas. A longitudinal study by Scheiner (2014) indicated for instance that participants in an online idea competition were generally aware of this issue and pointed to its possible and inherent negative consequences for participation. The remaining question is, however, at what point manipulation starts to harm the motivation of participation and when it starts to inhibit the intended objectives of VICs. Completely impeding manipulation is an unrealistic and unachievable endeavour. Participants will always explore and exploit ways to gain an advantage. Therefore, the main duty of developers and decision makers is to observe VICs for signs of manipulation and to decontaminate substantial threats for VICs.

The third obstacle and challenge arises from the so-called overjustification effect. The overjustification effect argues in general that external incentives can harm intrinsic motivation. Although it is still debated whether this effect truly exists (Lepper et al. 1999), the prevailing opinion assumes this negative effect. The work of Deci et al. (1999) especially convinced scholars and practitioners of this cause-effect relation. Deci et al. (1999) showed that 'tangible rewards had a sig-nificant negative effect on intrinsic motivation for interesting tasks, and this effect showed up with participants ranging from preschool to college, with interesting activities ranging from word games to construction puzzles, and with various rewards ranging from dollar bills to marshmallows' (p. 653). The use and imple-mentation of game design elements in VICs could subsequently influence the motivation of participations negatively.

5.6 Conclusion and Future Research

Although gamification describes an interesting and promising approach to enhance the experience in a VIC, its application includes obstacles and challenges. This section highlighted three important obstacles and challenges, which have to be considered when game design elements are included in VICs. But what would design elements for gamification in VICs that correspond, for example, with customers' fun and learning motivation look like? For instance, managers of VICs may define specific problems that go beyond customers' personal possibilities at first glance and thereby challenge customers to solve these problems by developing ideas. In this sense, it might be good to decompose these problems into various tasks, subtasks, and milestones. Users can solve such tasks by trial and error and repeat them until the problem is solved. This stimulates not only fun, but also learning through reaching particular skill levels after solving a task or subtask or reaching a milestone. In general, by designing tasks of increasing difficulty in applications of gamification, cognitive structures for the internalisation of learning contents may be systematically created, meaning learners enter a flow state and the above-outlined growth principle will be applied (Simões et al. 2013).

Another design element for gamification in VICs might be competition. Managers of VICs may organise idea competitions in the VIC for a defined, short runtime and call for ideas on a certain topic. An idea review committee could evaluate submitted ideas and by doing so determine the winner. Such idea competitions are not new in the scope of open innovation. For example, Leimeister et al. (2009) described how firms make use of idea competitions as a standalone instrument—as an alternative to a VIC—for integrating customers into the ideation for new product development. However, idea competitions as an integrated gamification concept for VICs are new. In this sense, idea competitions stimulate not only fun, but also learning by placing participants into the flow state.

References

Afuah, A. N., & Tucci, C. (2012). Crowdsourcing as a solution to distant search. *Academy of Management Review, 37*(3), 355–375.

Amabile, T. M. (1979). Effects of external evaluation on artistic creativity. *Journal of Personality and Social Psychology, 37*, 221–233.

Antikainen, M., Mäkipää, M., et al. (2010). Motivating and supporting collaboration in open innovation. *European Journal of Innovation Management, 13*(1), 100–119.

Belman, J., & Flanagan, M. (2010). Exploring the creative potential of values conscious game design: Students' experiences with the vap curriculum. *Eludamos. Journal for Computer Game Culture, 4*(1), 57–67.

Bessière, K., Seay, A. F., & Kiesler, S. (2007). The ideal elf: Identity exploration in world of warcraft. *CyberPsychology & Behavior, 10*(4), 530–535.

Bjork, S., & Holopainen, J. (2004). *Patterns in game design* (Game Development Series). Boston, MA: Charles River MediaOrt.

Blau, P. M. (1964). *Exchange and power in social life*. London: Transaction Publishers.

Blohm, I., & Leimeister, J. M. (2013). Gamification: Design of It-based enhancing services for motivational support and behavioral change. *Business & Information Systems Engineering, 5* (4), 275–278.

Bogost, I. (2011). Gamification is bullshit. http://bogost.com/writing/blog/gamification_is_bullshit/

Bretschneider, U., Leimeister, J. M., & Mathiassen, L. (2015). IT-enabled product innovation: Customer motivation for participating in virtual idea communities. *International Journal of Product Development, 20*(2), 126–141.

Bruner, J. S. (2009). *Actual minds, possible worlds*. London: Harvard University Press.

Buckler, S. A., & Zien, K. A. (1996). The spirituality of innovation: Learning from stories. *Journal of Product Innovation Management, 13*(5), 391–405.

Byrne, E. (2005). *Game level design*. Boston: Charles River Media.

Calvillo-Gámez, E. H., Cairns, P., & Cox, A. L. (2010). *Assessing the core elements of the gaming experience, evaluating user experience in games* (pp. 47–71). London: Springer.

Carroll, J. M. (1982). The adventure of getting to know a computer.*Computer 15*(11), 49–58.

Carroll, J. M., & Thomas, J. C. (1982). Metaphor and the cognitive representation of computing systems. *IEEE Transactions on Systems, Man, and Cybernetics, 12*(2), 107–116.

Chesbrough, H. (2003). The era of open innovation. *Sloan Management Review, 44*(4), 35–41.

Crumlish, C., & Malone, E. (2009). *Designing social interfaces: Principles, patterns, and practices for improving the user experience*. Sebastopol: O'Reilly Media Inc.

Dahan, E., & Hauser, J. R. (2002). The virtual customer. *Journal of Product Innovation Management, 19*(5), 332–353.

Danet, B., & Katriel, T. (1989). No two alike: Play and aesthetics in collecting. *Interpreting Objects and Collections, 2*(3), 253–277.

Deci, E. L., Koestner, R., & Ryan, R. M. (1999). A meta-analytic review of experiments examining the effects of extrinsic rewards on intrinsic motivation. *Psychological Bulletin, 125* (6), 627–668 (discussion 692–700).

Deterding, S., Dixon, D., Khaled, R., & Nacke, L. (2011). From game design elements to gamefulness: Defining gamification. In *Proceedings of the 15th International Academic MindTrek Conference: Envisioning Future Media Environments*: ACM (pp. 9–15).

Di Gangi, P. M., & Wasko, M. (2009). Steal my idea! organizational adoption of user innovations from a user innovation community: A case study of dell ideastorm. *Decision Support Systems, 48*, 303–312.

Frank, R. H. (1985). *Choosing the right pond: Human behavior and the quest for status*. New York: Oxford University Press.

Franke, N., & Piller, F. (2004). Value creation by toolkits for user innovation and design: The case of the watch market. *Journal of Product Innovation Management, 21*(6), 401–415.

Füller, J. (2006). Why consumers engage in virtual new product developments initiated by producers. *Advances in Consumer Research, 33*, 639–647.

Füller, J., Jawecki, G., & Mühlbacher, H. (2007). Innovation creation by online basketball communities. *Journal of Business Research, 60*(1), 60–71.

Fullerton, T. (2014). *Game design workshop: A playcentric approach to creating innovative games*. Burlington: Elsevier.

Fullerton, T., Swain, C., & Hoffman, S. (2004). *Game design workshop: Designing, prototyping, & playtesting games*. Lawrence: KS CMP Books.

Haas, P., Scheiner, C., Witt, M., Baccarella, C., & Leicht, N. (2013). Der Einfluss Von Gamification Auf Die Empfundene Selbstwirksamkeit Von Teilnehmern Von Online-Ideengenerierungswettbewerben Über Die Zeit, *GI-Jahrestagung*, 2321–2335.

Hacker, S., & Von Ahn, L. (2009). Matchin: Eliciting user preferences with an online game. In *Proceedings of the SIGCHI Conference on Human Factors in Computing Systems*: ACM (pp. 1207–1216).

Hamari, J., & Lehdonvirta, V. (2010). Game design as marketing: How game mechanics create demand for virtual goods. *International Journal of Business Science and Applied Management, 5*(1), 14–29.

Hassenzahl, M. (2004). The Thing and I: Understanding the relationship between user and product. In A. B. Mark, O. Kees, F. M. Andrew, & C. W. Peter (Eds.), *Funology* (pp. 31–42). Dordrecht: Kluwer Academic Publishers.

Henle, M. (1962). The birth and death of ideas. Contemporary approaches to creative thinking. In G. Gruber, G. Terrel, & M. Wertheimer (Eds.) (pp. 31–62). New York: Athrton.

Hoch, D., Roeding, C., & Lindner, S. K. (1999). *Secrets of software success.* Boston: Harvard Business School Press.

Holmström, B. (1999). Managerial incentive problems. A dynamic perspective. *Review of Economic Studies, 66,* 169–182.

Huotari, K., & Hamari, J. (2012). Defining gamification: A service marketing perspective. In *Proceeding of the 16th International Academic MindTrek Conference*: ACM (pp. 17–22).

Isbister, K., & Schaffer, N. (2008). *Game usability: Advancing the player experience.* London: CRC Press.

Jakobsson, M. (2002). Rest in peace, bill the bot: Death and life in virtual worlds. In *The social life of avatars* (pp. 63–76). London: Springer.

Jeppesen, L., & Frederiksen, L. (2006). Why do users contribute to firm-hosted user communities? The case of computer-controlled music instruments. *Organizational Science, 17*(1), 45–63.

Jokisch, M. (2007). *Active integration of users into the innovation process of a manufacturer: The BMW customer innovation lab.* Munich: Hut.

Lee, J. J., & Hammer, J. (2011). Gamification in education: What, how, why bother? *Academic Exchange Quarterly, 15*(2), 1–5.

Leimeister, J. M., Huber, M., Bretschneider, U., & Krcmar, H. (2009). Leveraging crowdsourcing: Activation-supporting components for it-based ideas competitions. *Journal of Management Information Systems, 26*(1), 197–224.

Lepper, M. R., Henderlong, J., & Gingras, I. (1999). Understanding the effects of extrinsic rewards on intrinsic motivation–uses and abuses of meta-analysis: Comment on Deci, E. L., Koestner, R., & Ryan, R. M. (1999). *Psychological Bulletin, 125*(6), 669–676 (discussion 692–700).

Long, M. M., & Schiffman, L. G. (1997). Swatch fever: An allegory for understanding the paradox of collecting. *Psychology & Marketing, 14*(5), 495–509.

Mallon, B., & Webb, B. (2000). Structure. *Causality, visibility and interaction: Propositions for evaluating engagement in narrative multimedia, international journal of human-computer studies, 53*(2), 269–287.

Malone, T. W. (1981). Toward a theory of intrinsically motivating instruction. *Cognitive Science, 5*(4), 333–369.

Maslow, A. H. (1987). *Motivation and personality.* New York: Harper.

McGuire, M., & Jenkins, O. C. (2008). *Creating games: Mechanics, content, and technology.* Wellesley: A. K. Peters Ltd./CRC Press.

McKenna, K. Y., & Bargh, J. A. (2000). Plan 9 from cyberspace: The implications of the internet for personality and social psychology. *Personality and Social Psychology Review, 4*(1), 57–75.

Motzek, R. (2007). *Motivation in open innovation: An exploratory study on user innovators.* Saarbrücken: VDM.

Nambisan, S. (2002). Designing virtual customer environments for new product development: Toward a theory. *Academy of Management Review, 27*(3), 392–413.

Petkov, P., Köbler, F., Foth, M., Medland, R., & Krcmar, H. (2011). Engaging energy saving through motivation-specific social comparison. In *CHI'11 Extended Abstracts on Human Factors in Computing Systems*: ACM (pp. 1945–1950).

Piller, F. T., & Walcher, D. (2006). Toolkits for idea competitions: A novel method to integrate users in new product development. *R&D Management, 36*(3), 307–318.

Reeves, B., & Read, J. L. (2009). *Total engagement: Using games and virtual worlds to change the way people work and businesses compete.* New York: Harvard Business Review Press.

Salen, K., & Zimmerman, E. (2004). *Rules of play: Game design fundamentals*. Cambridge: MIT University Press Group Ltd.

Schattke, K., Seeliger, J., Schiepe-Tiska, A., & Kehr, H. M. (2012). Activity-related incentives as motivators in open innovation communities. *International Journal of Knowledge-Based Organizations, 2*(1), 21–34.

Scheiner, C. W. (2015). The motivational fabric of gamified idea competitions: The evaluation of game mechanics from a longitudinal pespective. *Creativity and Innovation Management, 24* (2), 341–352.

Scheiner, C. (2014). The motivational fabric of gamified idea competitions–the evaluation of game mechanics from a longitudinal perspective. *Creativity and Innovation Management, 24*(2), 341–352.

Scheiner, C. W., & Witt, M. (2013). The backbone of gamification-a theoretical consideration of play and game mechanics. *GI-Jahrestagung*, 2372–2386.

Schell, J. (2008). *The art of game design*. Burlington: Morgan Kaufmann Publishers.

Simões, J., Redondo, R. D., & Vilas, A. F. (2013). A social gamification framework for a K-6 learning platform. *Computers in Human Behavior, 29*(2), 345–353.

Sun, C.-T., Lin, H., & Ho, C. H. (2006). Sharing tips with strangers: Exploiting gift culture in computer gaming. *CyberPsychology & Behavior, 9*(5), 560–570.

Taylor, T. (2009). The assemblage of play. *Games and Culture, 4*(4), 331–339.

Thompson, J., Berbank-Green, B., & Cusworth, N. (2007). *Game design: Principles, practice, and techniques-the ultimate guide for the aspiring game designer*. Hoboken: Wiley.

Von Ahn, L., & Dabbish, L. (2008). Designing games with a purpose. *Communications of the ACM, 51*(8), 58–67.

Werbach, K., & Hunter, D. (2012). *For the win: how game thinking can revolutionize your business*. Philadelphia: Wharton Digital Press.

Witt, M., Scheiner, C., Robra-Bissantz, S., & Voigt, K.-I. (2012). Creative process engagement in a multiplayer online ideation game. *GI-Jahrestagung*, 978–991.

Zhang, P. (2008). Technical opinion motivational affordances: Reasons for Ict design and use. *Communications of the ACM, 51*(11), 145–147.

Chapter 6
Boundaries of Open Innovation and Games

Maximilian Witt

Abstract Over the past decade, systems that are used to support the early phases of the innovation process have evolved from simple suggestion boxes to sophisticated social media platforms for the development and refinement of ideas. Organisations who want to profit from the use of these platforms face the following two significant and interconnected challenges: First, organisations have to motivate (groups of) individuals to participate, and they must place them in a state of high involvement and flow. Second, organisations must inspire individuals in order to generate creative output. One activity that leads to high motivation, to a feeling of flow and involvement, and to creative output, is play. This chapter focuses on the question of how to design social media based on open innovation tools to harness the potential of play by applying game mechanics to innovation management. It is argued that there are two possibilities: either enriching open innovation tools with game mechanics (*gamification*) or adjusting a multiplayer online game to the purpose of ideation (*online ideation game*). This chapter sheds light on these two possibilities and gives practical implications for implementation. The first section of this chapter describes how specific game mechanics can be implemented in social media based on open innovation tools. The second section of this chapter illustrates a number of online ideation games that have recently been applied and shows how the previous described game mechanics can also serve as building blocks for those games. The third section of this chapter gives managers key lessons at hand who strive to apply game mechanics to innovation management. The key lessons relate to (1) the *planning and design* phase and (2) the *introduction and operation* phase of a gamified open innovation tool or an online ideation game.

This contribution has already been published as part of the authors Ph.D-Thesis at Technische Universität Carolo-Wilhemnia zu Braunschweig, 2013: Witt, M.: Application of Game Mechanics to Innovation Management. Theoretical Foundations and Empirical Studies, available at: http://digisrv-1.biblio.etc.tu-bs.de:8080/docportal/servlets/MCRFileNodeServlet/DocPortal_derivate_00029356/ediss.pdf;jsessionid=5A06F13AC981960D905E3E200DBB5E57.

M. Witt (✉)
Telefonica Germany GmbH & Co OHG, Munich, Germany
e-mail: maximilian.witt@telefonica.com

© Springer International Publishing Switzerland 2017
S. Stieglitz et al. (eds.), *Gamification*, Progress in IS,
DOI 10.1007/978-3-319-45557-0_6

6.1 Introduction

The use of social media platforms for the development and refinement of ideas has occurred not only as a result of technological developments, but also because of a paradigm shift from a closed to an open innovation model. Accessing the potential of individuals within and outside organisations has become the threshold for the existence of organisations, and offers opportunities for gaining a competitive advantage (e.g., Chesbrough 2003; Robra-Bissantz and Lattemann 2005). With the possibilities currently offered by the World Wide Web, the main challenges are not accessibility, but rather the design of social media based on open innovation tools such as idea competitions or toolkits. Regarding the design, organisations seeking to profit from the use of the tools face the following two significant and inter-connected challenges (Füller 2009; Adamczyk et al. 2010): First, organisations have to motivate individuals to participate, and they must place them in a state of high involvement and flow (Robra-Bissantz and Lattemann 2005). Second, organisations must inspire individuals in order to generate creative output, as cre-ativity is the main prerequisite for the ability 'to make valuable and innovative contributions to a firm's new product development process' (Füller 2010, p. 104).

One activity that leads to high motivation, to a feeling of flow and involvement, and to creative output, is play (e.g., Csikszentmihalyi 1990). The influence of play on creativity and motivation has been widely recognised. Specifically, neuroscience has demonstrated that play is an important enticement mechanism of human behaviour, and is responsible for the emission of neurochemicals that influence development of the social brain and the neural network (e.g., Panksepp and Burgdorf 2003). Researchers from social science and psychology (e.g., Dansky 1980a) have proposed that play is the child's first creative act, and it stimulates free association, fluidity of thinking and mental transformation. These authors also showed that play allows the release of negative affect and results in positive affect (such as enjoyment and relaxation). As early as the eighteenth century, the philosopher Kant (1787) defined play as the connection between experience and thinking. And the philosopher von Schiller argued that a person must play in order to do valuable work. More recent organisational literature has shown that play can help to improve the product design process (Schrage 2000), engage people in learning (e.g., Statler et al. 2009) and in strategy development processes (Jacobs and Heracleous 2006). In the field of innovation management, however, the concept of play is relatively new (Mainemelis and Ronson 2006).

This contribution focuses on the question of how to design social media based on open innovation tools to harness the potential of play. Accordingly, the ideas from authors such as Zichermann and Linder (2010) and Reeves and Read (2009) are emphasised who suggested that the application of game design elements, that is, game mechanics such as points, levels and leaderboards, can help to take advantage of the potential of play. It is argued that there are two possibilities for applying game mechanics to innovation management—either by enriching open innovation tools with game mechanics (*gamification*) or by adjusting a multiplayer online game to the purpose of ideation (*online ideation game*). Although research has begun to acknowledge the benefits of enriching open innovation tools with game mechanics (Leimeister et al. 2009) and of developing *online ideation games* (OIGs) (Füller et al. 2010), comparatively little research has been conducted in this context.

This chapter addresses this research gap by shedding light on two possibilities for applying game mechanics to innovation management and providing implications for practical use. The next section describes how specific game mechanics can be implemented in social media based on open innovation tools. Section 6.2 illustrates a number of OIGs that have recently been applied and shows how the previous described game mechanics can also serve as building blocks for those games. Section 6.3 gives managers key lessons at hand, who strive to apply game mechanics to innovation management. The key lessons relate to (1) the *planning and design phase* and (2) the *introduction and operation* phase of a gamified open innovation tool or an OIG.

6.2 Possibilities for Applying Game Mechanics to Innovation Management

In this chapter gamification is addressed first and OIGs second for two interrelated reasons: First, game mechanics have already been applied to open innovation tools for a number of years, while OIGs have been realised for only a short time. Second, while gamified open innovation tools appear to be of low gamefullnes, OIGs are of high gamefulness. *Gamefulness* describes the extent to which the design of a system appears to be a game (McGonigal 2011):

> Where 'playfulness' broadly denotes the experiential and behavioural qualities of playing (paidia), 'gamefulness' denotes the qualities of gaming (ludus) (Deterding et al. 2011a).

The order of the application possibilities, therefore, reflects the evolution of open innovation tools from *non-gameful* tools, to *gameful* tools, to games. Figure 6.1. (own figure) illustrates this evolution.

6.2.1 Gamification

Gamification is defined as the application of game design elements to a non-game context (Deterding et al. 2011b). *Game design* is thereby defined as 'the process by which a game designer creates a game, to be encountered by a player, from which meaningful play emerges' (Salen and Zimmerman 2004, p. 80). *Game design elements* are characteristics of games and comprise terms such as game mechanics and so-called 'game design heuristics' (such as challenge, fantasy and curiosity) (Malone 1982). *Application in a non-game context* means that these game design

Fig. 6.1 Evolution of open innovation tools (own figure)

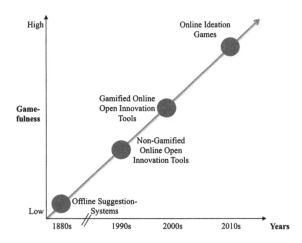

elements are used 'for other purposes than their normal expected use for entertainment' (Deterding et al. 2011b, p. 3).

The following section describes how game mechanics can be implemented in social media based on open innovation tools. Therefore, specific examples of *idea competitions* and *idea management systems* that are used in the automotive industry serve as a helpful illustration.

One possibility for structuring the described game mechanics in the context of innovation management is the *genex framework* (Shneiderman 1999; Leimeister et al. 2009). According to this framework, efficient creativity-supporting software tools must encourage four generic behaviours: accumulating, relating, creating and disseminating. The generic behaviour '*accumulation*' refers to learning from previous work, as well as searching, browsing, validating and indexing information. The generic behaviour '*relating*' implies behaviours such as consulting with peers and mentors. The generic behaviour '*creation*' relates to behaviours such as exploring and creating possible solutions. The generic behaviour '*dissemination*' describes the behaviour of spreading, and thereby contributing, information and elaborated solutions (Shneiderman 1999).

Game points can serve as triggers for all four behaviours. They can be assigned to activities such as tagging information (*accumulating*); commenting, leaving a message for someone, rating an idea or connecting to peers (*relating*); developing an idea by adding further information or creating videos or pictures of prototypes (*creating*); or posting (i.e., publishing) the idea (*disseminating*). For example, in VW's idea competition *App My Ride*, participants could earn game points for commenting on an idea, leaving a message for another member, rating and submitting an idea.

Social points can serve as triggers for the generic behaviour '*relating*', as they are a way to gather feedback from, and thus consult with, others. An idea competition in the automotive industry for which social points were assigned was BMW's *Interior Idea Contest*. Participants could evaluate ideas from other participants by clicking '*thumbs-up*' or '*thumbs-down*' on two dimensions ('I like this idea' and 'I would use this service'). Diverse evaluation dimensions are applied, including dimensions such as originality, degree of innovation, marketing potentials or customer value (Leimeister et al. 2009; Möslein et al. 2010). In open innovation tools, assessment through social points is labelled *open evaluation* (Möslein et al. 2010), *community rating* (Leimeister et al. 2009) or *group decision* (Malone et al. 2009).

Redeemable points can serve as triggers for generic behaviours '*creating*' and '*relating*'. For example, in the idea management systems of Hype (www. hypeinnovation.com) and Spigit (www.spigit.com), two of the largest idea management system providers worldwide, users can spend their earned points in a *virtual store*. In these virtual stores, innovators can redeem their points for money or monetary compensation (such as a holiday trip). Monetary compensation does not necessarily mean a reward that can be converted outside the company or the innovation tool. In some systems the innovators can instruct professional designers to sketch or to build a prototype of their idea by paying them with redeemable points. The designers take pictures of sketches and prototypes to upload into the system. Therefore, redeemable points can be assigned to the behaviour of *creating*, because they help participants to create their ideas. The Spigit idea management system also gives participants the option to invest their points in the ideas that they find most promising. Participants who buy shares of the ideas that are selected for further development or implementation are rewarded with additional redeemable points, which indicates that this approach also allows for evaluating ideas. Therefore, redeemable points can also serve as triggers for *relating* behaviours, as they are a way to gather feedback from, and thus consult with, others.

Levels that can be implemented in the form of sections or stages can serve as triggers for the behaviours '*accumulating*' and/or '*creating*'. When levels are implemented in the form of sections, they imply the possibility of browsing through information (and thus support *accumulating*). For example, in the idea management system of Hype, users can choose to take part in different campaigns. A campaign is a single challenge that focuses on one topic. Different campaigns do not have to be approached gradually by users and can be interpreted as a level in the form of a section. When levels are implemented in the form of stages, they, for example, gradually give innovators the opportunity to work on ideas in the later stages of the innovation process and provide ever-increasing challenges. Therefore, levels in the form of stages relate to *creating*, because users have to explore and create new solutions in order to move up a level. Levels in the form of stages, however, are either not applied or are applied only in a limited way in open innovation tools that are available on the market.

Leaderboards can serve as triggers for the genex framework behaviours *accumulating* and *relating*, as they support behaviours such as searching, browsing, and consulting with others. *App My Ride* can again serve as an example for an open innovation tool with a leaderboard. In *App My Ride*, a ranking list shows participants how they perform in comparison to others in the categories of *idea generation, evaluation* and *development*. The leaderboards can be sorted and browsed according to the following criteria: (1) activity-counter, (2) number of comments, (3) number of evaluations, (4) number of messages and (5) number of ideas.

Collecting, which is also only marginally applied to open innovation tools, can be assigned to the behaviour of *accumulating*, as it is a way to gather information about the submitted ideas of others: In some idea competitions (e.g., in BMW's *Interior Idea Contest*) participants have an opportunity to show others their collections of generated ideas.

Exchange can be assigned to the behaviours *relating* and *disseminating*, because it relates to gathering information from peers and mentors (*relating*) and to publishing information (e.g., in a forum) (*disseminating*). For example, in VW's *People's Car Project*, participants could help each other with ideas by commenting and sharing thoughts.

Stories can be assigned to the generic behaviour of *creating* and *disseminating*: Ideas can be created and published in the form of a dynamic, unplanned and interactive story. For example, in BMW's *Interior Idea Contest* or in VW's *People's Car Project*, participants had an opportunity to write and share their ideas in the form of stories (e.g., in a blog or in a wiki).

Virtual identity can be assigned to the behaviour of *relating*: In all named idea competitions, participants could generate a visual representation of themselves within the system, and could contact and consult with other community members through their virtual identities.

6.2.2 (Multiplayer) OIG

The second possibility for applying game mechanics to innovation management is the use of a multiplayer online game for the purpose of ideation. A *multiplayer OIG* gives players the opportunity to solve real-world problems within a game environment. Thus, an OIG follows the idea of 'games with a purpose, i.e., games that are fun to play and at the same time collect useful data for tasks that computers cannot yet perform' (Hacker and von Ahn 2009, p. 2). A few researchers (e.g., Hacker and von Ahn 2009; Cooper et al. 2010; Füller et al. 2010) have recently demonstrated that online games have the potential to motivate people to deliver useful data. However, the utilisation of online games for integrating individuals into ideation has been, to date, almost completely ignored in scientific research. One plausible explanation for this research deficit is that, since the dawn of the Industrial Revolution, playing games has been viewed as superfluous or even hazardous for adults (Spariosu 1989). *Play* was and is often described as the opposite of work (Mainemelis and Ronson 2006). From this perspective, an *ideation game* is an oxymoron: according to the French social thinker Roger Caillois (1961) playing a game is separate from the real world and is non-productive. In contrast to playing a game, ideation relates to the solution of real-world problems and is undertaken to achieve a specific outcome (i.e., the generation of creative ideas). An OIG, then, appears to encounter the same critiques as game-based learning did in its early days

(Garris et al. 2002): Critics pointed out that harnessing the potential of games for instructional purposes squeezes out what is enjoyable about games in the first place. However, a number of OIGs have recently been applied to solve real-world problems. Examples of OIGs include *MMOWGLI* (www.mmowgli.nps.edu), *Foldit* (http://fold.it), *Breakthroughs to Cures* (http://breakthroughstocures.org) or *Catalysts for Change* (http://catalyze4change.org):

MMOWGLI *MMOWGLI* is an acronym for 'Massive Multiplayer Online War Game Leveraging the Internet'. Using the game *MMOWGLI*, the United States Navy sought to explore whether players of a multiplayer online game can solve complex geopolitical problems, i.e., how to deal with piracy in the Gulf of Aden. The game, which was launched in June 2011 and ran for three weeks, was sponsored by the Office of Naval Research and was developed cooperatively by the Institute for the Future (IFTF) and the Naval Postgraduate School (NPS). In this game, which runs on any web-browser, ideas are labelled as *cards*. Players can play cards and can build *card chains* by collaborating with other players and thus form larger sets of ideas. By building on these card chains, an *action plan* is jointly developed among the players. Masters moderate the game progress.

Foldit *Foldit* is a game that was developed at the University of Washington from computer science and engineering departments in collaboration with the department of biochemistry. It was launched in the year 2008 and has been playable since that time. In *Foldit* players help to develop ideas for the folding of proteins. These ideas can help lead to a cure for diseases such as HIV, cancer and Alzheimer's (Cooper et al. 2010). In the game, players focus on creating accurate protein structure models. Players change protein structures with a variety of tools and manipulations, and share their strategies as *recipes* in a social media based environment. Other players can advance developed recipes.

Breakthroughs to Cures In *Breakthroughs to Cures*, players generated ideas about the enhancement of the medical research system and about drug development. The game was hosted by the Myelin Repair Foundation (MRF). It was funded through a grant from the Robert Wood Johnson Foundation's Pioneer Portfolio and developed by the Institute for the Future (IFTF). Uniquely, this game was available for play only twice, and only for 48 h each time (from October 7 to 8, 2010, and from November 9 to 10, 2010). The game is similar to *MMOWGLI*: After watching a video, participants can play 'positive imagination' and 'critical imagination' cards. One card is limited to 140 characters. Cards can be seen in a stream (similar to the micro-blog Twitter). Players can build card chains, which means to debate, extend and pose questions about the generated ideas.

Catalysts for Change The goal of *Catalysts for Change* is to 'identify new paths out of poverty in just 48 h of gameplay with hundreds of players from all walks of life'. With this basis, the "*game invites players to share their own ideas for helping the destitute or to build upon more than 600 ideas that have been already created by 11 non-profit groups from all around the world*" (Takahashi 2012). It was also developed by the IFTF and supported by the Rockefeller Foundation, and could be played for 48 h only: From April 3 to April 5, 2012.

The specific examples of OIGs, and OIGs in general, can be classified with respect to the following two design elements:

- **Mission specificity** OIGs provide players with mission goals to solve. Mission topics can be either very specific or very broad. An example of a game with very specific missions is *Foldit*. *MMOWGLI*, *Breakthroughs to Cures* and *Catalysts for Change* are examples of OIGs with broader missions.
- **Duration** While some OIGs do not have a time limit, others have a predefined duration. *Foldit* is one example of a game without a time limit (Cooper et al. 2010). The OIGs *Breakthroughs to Cures* and *Catalysts for Change*, on the other hand, had a duration of only 48 h, and had to be completed within that time limit.

MMOWGLI, *Foldit*, *Breakthroughs to Cures* and *Catalysts for Change* also allow exemplifying how game points, social points, levels, leaderboards, collecting, exchange and stories can serve as building blocks for the OIGs, thereby covering behaviours of the genex framework.

Game points serve as triggers in the investigated OIGs for *relating* (commenting, leaving a message to someone or rating an idea), *creating* and *disseminating* (generating and publishing an idea). For example, in *MMOWGLI* players can earn game points for becoming an author of an action plan, for adding a comment or rating an action plan. Game points are also multiplied if the game masters rate a player's action plan as one of the top five plans, or if a player has added five comments to a plan that is positively evaluated.

Social points serve as triggers in the investigated OIGs for *relating*: For example, MMOWGLI players also get a social point if they consult with other players—that is, other players build on their cards. In *Catalysts for Change* players also received explicit social points when someone marked the idea as interesting.

Levels serve as triggers in the investigated OIGs for *accumulating* and *creating*. An example for an OIG with levels in the form of two stages is *Foldit*. In the *Intro Levels* players learn the rules of the game, as well as learning how to fold and how to create an accurate protein structure model (*accumulating*). In the *Science Levels*, players are able to fold a variety of different proteins with a scientifically unknown structure (Cooper et al. 2010). In contrast to *Foldit*, *Catalysts for Change* has a level system that is connected to the points system: The more points *Catalysts for Change*-players earn, the faster they level up. Therefore, they relate to *creating*, because players have to explore and create new solutions to level up.

Leaderboards serve as triggers in the investigated OIGs for *accumulating* and *relating*, because they evoke behaviours such as searching and browsing, as well as consulting with others. *Foldit* is also an example of an OIG with a leaderboard: A ranking list shows players how they perform in relation to others (Witt et al. 2011b).

Collecting (e.g., badges, awards or achievements) is a further game mechanism that can be found in OIGs. Collecting serves as a trigger in the investigated OIGs for *accumulating*, *creating* and *relating*. For example, in *MMOWGLI* four badges can be earned for such actions as starting the longest card chain in a move or earning the most points in a move. Therefore, collecting badges relates to *creating*, because players have to explore and create new solutions in order to receive badges. In *Catalysts for Change* three types of awards can be earned: automatic awards, game guide awards and celebrity awards. The awards can be shown to others and thus evoke behaviours such as searching and browsing (*accumulating*). Additionally, collecting can be assigned to the behaviour *relating* of the genex framework, because the game guide awards and celebrity awards support consulting with peers and experts.

Exchange serves as triggers in the investigated OIGs for *creating*, *disseminating* and *relating*. In *MMOWGLI*, *Breakthroughs to Cures* or *Catalysts for Change*, for example, players can comment on ideas or contribute to an action plan (*creating* and *disseminating*). In *Foldit*, players can chat with each other and discuss how *recipes* should be elaborated (*relating*) (Cooper et al. 2010).

Stories can serve as triggers in the investigated OIGs for *accumulating*, *creating* and *disseminating*. In *Breakthroughs to Cures* both types of stories are implemented: (1) dynamic, unplanned and interactive stories and (2) static, predefined and passive stories. The first type appears as players have the possibility to write a story on their own and thus influence the game itself. For example, players of *Breakthroughs to Cures* have the opportunity to write a story on their own, and thereby influence the game itself through dynamic, unplanned and interactive stories. These stories allow exploring/composing and publishing ideas, and in this way relate to the generic behaviour of *creating* and *disseminating*. In the background story of *Breakthrough to Cures*, a futuristic scenario that takes place in 2020 is presented: A widespread contamination has triggered a neurological disease that is expected to infect hundreds of millions of people. The background story supports the collection of information and thus can be assigned to *accumulating*.

6.3 Implications for Practice

Synthesising the insights gained by the author of this work (e.g., Witt et al. 2011b, 2012a), a set of *key lessons* can be generated. These key lessons not only can help managers who strive to apply game mechanics to innovation management, but they are a necessary condition for the successful application of game mechanics. The key lessons relate to (1) the *planning and design phase* and (2) the *introduction and operation phase* of a gamified open innovation tool or an OIG.

6.3.1 (1) Planning and Design Phase

The lessons to be recognised from the design phase do follow (1) a structured process, (2) provide clearly defined goals, (3) minimise the risk of fraud and (4) create an environment characterised by high usability.

(1) **Follow a structured process** The application of game mechanics often carried out is poorly conceived and inadequate. A structured process can help to apply game mechanics in an effective way (Kim 2010). Before applying game mechanics to innovation management, as a first step the aims of the system must be defined. Thus, innovation managers must answer the following question: What shall be accomplished with the open innovation tool or OIG? Whether using a gamified system or the OIG, innovation managers must gain a clear understanding of how many ideas they want to have generated and commercialised as short-, middle- and long-term objectives. In a second step, innovation managers have to determine all possible activities that are, from their perspective, important for effective ideation within the system. Examples for such activities are *post an idea, log in, finish tutorial, give other participants advice, refer to a similar idea, post a comment, enlarge virtual identity, visit virtual identity, suggest a campaign, suggest an expert, rate an idea.* In a third step, innovation managers must rank the activities determined in the second step according to their importance. As a fourth step of the process, motives of targeted innovators have to be investigated, and in a fifth step managers must choose and align game mechanics so that motives and, accordingly, behaviours are triggered.

(2) **Provide clearly defined goals** Players of an OIG want to have clearly defined and formulated missions and goals. When goals are too fuzzy, participants tend to be overextended and frustrated (Witt et al. 2012a). One possibility for specifying missions and goals—and thus motivate participants—is using background stories in the form of comics such as those found in the OIG *Evoke.* Stories can provide information in order to clarify the topic. However, it is central to many users that this information is perceived as useful for the solution of missions; otherwise, they will quickly lose interest in reading the stories.

(3) **Minimise the risk of fraud** It is important to anticipate and minimise the risk of fraud when designing a gamified open innovation tool or an OIG (Scheiner and Witt 2012). Therefore, designers have to think carefully about which kind of undesirable behaviour the application and the configuration of game mechanics can evoke (Dellarocas 2011). For example, before deciding to allocate game points for posting an idea or comments, designers should consider that users might disregard the quality of their contributions and might post just to boost their scores or the numbers of collected badges. The same applies for social points: Participants might act in rating gangs or use unfair rating strategies to enhance their reputation within the system. Fraud can make using the system less enjoyable for participants and can be detrimental to a game (Salen and Zimmerman 2004). As it is, in general, impossible to create a gamified system or game that is totally fraud-resistant (Salen and Zimmerman 2004), a few strategies (detailed as follows) can help to minimise the risk.

There are three dimensions that can influence the fraud-resistance of a gamified system or an OIG, and must be considered in the design phase (e.g., Dellarocas 2011).

1. The larger the efforts and the more time necessary to cheat, the lower the probability of fraud.

The effort and time necessary to cheat can be increased with a number of strategies. For example, users receive game points depending on their trustworthiness-level (Farmer 2011). Trustworthiness of a user can be calculated either by 'rating-the-rater' or by using meta-data about a user's behaviour (Lampe 2011). In this way, gaining game points for spam-like postings becomes more difficult. Likewise, social points (for example) are only allocated if a certain number of persons—persons who have not evaluated the user's last ideas—rated the idea positively. This increases the effort and time necessary to act in rating gangs, and thus exacerbates efforts to cheat. Both this increase in complexity and the increase in control, however, have a downside as either can lessen a site's credibility and usability.

2. The more transparent the rules are, the easier it is for cheaters to find strategies for cheating.

Concealing the details about such aspects regarding how game points and social points are allocated, or exactly when a new level can be reached, or how a user can reach a higher position in the leaderboard is another possibility for resisting fraud in open innovation tools or OIGs. As an example, concealing details is a strategy used by Amazon and Google for their rankings list. Dellarocas (2011) highlights in this regard that Amazon *does not disclose the precise formula they use to rank-order reviewers* and Google *does not disclose all the details of rank-ordering search results* (p. 9). However, designers have to be aware that lack of transparency has disadvantages as well: Concealing (feedback) information provided by game mechanics can hinder users, diminishing their ability to learn and lowering their trust in the system and in a site's credibility (Dellarocas 2011).

3. The more the true identity of a user is known, the lower the probability of fraud.

When virtual identities are completely anonymous and are easy to create, users are able to generate fake identities and spam the system with low-quality contributions and fabricated ratings (Scheiner et al. 2012). Mapping virtual and real identities can help to reduce such behaviours. To counter privacy concerns, real identity characteristics do not have to be visible to every community member, but could be available only to administrators of the system. When mapping virtual and real identities, however, designers also have to be aware of the potential disadvantages. The tactics can discourage users from joining the system, can cause users to post only positive feedback and can increase reporting bias (Dellarocas 2011). Thus, identity mapping can have a negative influence on constructs such as equality and divergent thinking.

When deciding how to balance these dimensions, designers have to take context information (e.g., motives of participants, or business culture) into account.

(4) **Create an environment characterised by high usability** In the *design phase*, usability considerations hold great importance. Game mechanics open up their potential only if the system provides intuitive usage, and a clear and individually adjusted navigation structure. For example, leaderboards must be easy to find and clearly presented—participants need to be able to quickly see themselves in the rankings list without clicking through a long list.

6.3.2 (2) Introduction and Operation Phase

The lessons contributed by the *introduction and operation phase* are '*care for the community*' and '*evaluate and improve application*' of game mechanics.

Care for the community In many cases a vibrant community is an essential prerequisite of an effective, gamified open innovation tool or OIG: Social points are given by other participants, leaderboards show the position of a user in relation to other participants, and exchange takes on characteristics of communication between participants. Because of this emphasis on the relationships among participants, continuous management and support of the community is necessary. This task is time-consuming and cost-intensive, and must have support from top management (Hutter et al. 2010). Care, therefore, is essential to creating success through a gamified open innovation tool or an OIG community.

Evaluate and improve application of game mechanics Testing the effect of game mechanics iteratively is not only important for the design phase, but also for the introduction and operation phase. Opinions about and behavioural patterns in response to game mechanics are often difficult to foresee. While testing and evaluating, designers can encounter problems such as a need to improve the design of leaderboards, game points that have to be more difficult to reach, for instance social points and badges might need a more balanced increase in level of difficulty.

6.4 Summary

This chapter argued that there are two possibilities for applying game mechanics to innovation management. One possibility is enriching open innovation tools with game mechanics (*gamification*), and the second is using, for the purpose of ideation, a game (*OIG*) in which game mechanics are used as building blocks. Although research has begun to acknowledge the benefits of enriching open innovation tools with game mechanics, as well as the benefits that play holds for open innovation, comparatively little research has been conducted in this context. Results of this contribution can be summarised as follows.

The first section described how specific game mechanics (such as game points, social points, levels and leaderboards) are implemented in social media based on open innovation tools. It was shown that game mechanics serve as triggers for the four generic behaviours efficient creativity-supporting software tools must encourage according to the 'genex framework' (Shneiderman 1999; Leimeister et al. 2009): accumulating, relating, creating and disseminating.

The second section illustrated a number of OIGs (such as *MMOWGLI*, *Foldit* or *Breakthrough to Cures*) that have recently been applied. Game mechanics, as described in the first section, were also identified within these games and were mapped to the generic behaviours of the 'genex framework'.

The third section provided managers with key lessons at hand for (1) the *planning and design phase* and (2) the *introduction and operation phase*, who strive to apply game mechanics to innovation management. In the planning phase and design phase managers should strive to follow a structured process by gaining a clear understanding of how many ideas they want to have generated, which activities are from high, mid or low importance for effective ideation and how they can motivate these activities. Managers should also provide clearly defined goals, should anticipate and minimise the risk of fraud when designing a gamified open innovation tool or an OIG, and create an environment characterised by high usability. In the introduction and operation phase managers have to continuously manage and support the ideation community and also improve the application of game mechanics.

References

Adamczyk, S., Bullinger, A. C. & Möslein, K. M. (2010). *Call for attention—attracting and activating innovators.* Paper presented at the R&D Management Conference, 30 June–2 July, Manchester, http://wi1.uni-erlangen.de/sites/wi1.uni-erlangen.de/files/Adamczyk_Bullinger__Moeslein_Call_for_Attention_RDMgmt2010.pdf

Caillois, R. (1961). *Man, play, and games* (M. Barash, Trans., 2001). New York: Free Press of Glencoe.

Chesbrough, H. W. (2003). The era of open innovation. *MIT Sloan Management Review, 44*(3), 35–42.

Cooper, S., Khatib, F., Treuille, A., Barbero, J., Lee, J., Beenen, M., et al. (2010). Predicting protein structures with a multiplayer online game. *Nature, 466*(7307), 756–760.

Csikszentmihalyi, M. (1990). *Flow: The psychology of optimal experience.* New York: Harper and Row.

Dansky, J. L. (1980). Cognitive consequences of sociodramatic play and exploration training for economically disadvantaged preschoolers. *Journal of Child Psychology and Psychiatry, 21*(1), 47–58.

Dellarocas, C. (2011). Designing reputation systems for the social web. In H. Masum & M. Tovey (Eds.), *The reputation society. How online opinions are reshaping the offline world* (pp. 3–11). Cambridge, Massachusetts: MIT Press.

Deterding, S., Dixon, D., Khaled, R. & Nacke, L. (2011a). *From game design elements to gamefulness: Defining gamification.* Paper presented at the MindTrek'11 Conference, 28–30 September, Tampere, Finland, https://www.cs.auckland.ac.nz/courses/compsci747s2c/lectures/paul/definition-deterding.pdf. Accessed 14 January 2016.

Deterding, S., Khaled, R., Nacke, L. E. & Dixon, D. (2011b). *Gamification: Toward a definition.* In Paper presented at the CHI 2011 Workshop Gamification, 7–11 May, Vancouver, BC, Canada, http://gamification-research.org/wp-content/uploads/2011/04/CHI_2011_Gamification_Work shop.pdf. Accessed 14 January 2016.

Farmer, R. (2011). Web reputation systems and the real world. In H. Masum, & M. Tovey (Eds.), *The reputation society. How online opinions are reshaping the offline world* (pp. 13–24). Cambridge, Massachusetts: MIT Press.

Füller, J. (2009). Anleitung zum Kreativsein. *Harvard Business Manager, 9*, 98–101.

Füller, J. (2010). Refining virtual co-creation from a consumer perspective. *California Management Review, 52*(2), 98–123.

Füller, J., Möslein, K. M., Hutter, K. & Haller, J. B. A. (2010). Evaluation games—how to make the crowd your jury. In K. P. Fähnrich & B. Franczyk (Eds.), *Lecture notes informatics (LNI) proceedings*, P-175 (pp. 955–960).

Garris, R., Ahlers, R., & Driskell, J. E. (2002). Games, motivation, and learning: A research and practice model. *Simulation & Gaming, 33*(4), 441–467.

Hacker, S., & von Ahn, L. (2009). Matchin: Eliciting user preferences with an online game, In *Proceedings of the 27th International Conference on Human Factors in Computing Systems in Boston, Massachusetts, 2009,* (pp. 1207–1216). ACM: New York.

Hutter, K., Hautz, J., Füller, J., Matzler, K., & Mayr, A. (2010). Ideenwettbewerbe als innovatives Markenbindungsinstrument. *Marketing Review St. Gallen, 27*(4), 26–34.

Jacobs, C., & Heracleous, L. T. (2006). Constructing shared understanding: The role of embodied metaphors in organization development. *Journal of Applied Behavioral Science, 42*(2), 207–226.

Kant, I. (1787). *Critique of pure reason* (J. M. D. Meiklejohn, Trans., 1950). The Pennsylvania State University. http://www2.hn.psu.edu/faculty/jmanis/kant/Critique-Pure-Reason.pdf. Accessed 14 January 2016.

Kim, A. J. (2010). Gamification workshop. http://www.slideshare.net/amyjokim/gamification-workshop-2010

Lampe, C. (2011). The role of reputation systems in managing online communities. In H. Masum & M. Tovey (Eds.), *The reputation society. How online opinions are reshaping the offline world* (pp. 13–24). Cambridge, Massachusetts: MIT Press.

Leimeister, J. M., Huber, M., Bretschneider, U., & Krcmar, H. (2009). Leveraging crowdsourcing —theory-driven design, implementation and evaluation of activation-supporting components for IT-based idea competitions. *Journal of Management Information Systems, 26*(1), 197–224.

Mainemelis, C., & Ronson, S. (2006). Ideas are born in fields of play: Towards a theory of play and creativity in organizational settings. *Research in Organizational Behavior, 27*(6), 81–131.

Malone, T. W. (1982). Heuristics for designing enjoyable user interfaces: Lessons from computer games. In *Proceedings of the 1982 Conference on Human Factors in Computing Systems* (pp. 63–68). Gaithersburg, Maryland, 1982, ACM: Washington D.C.

Malone, T. W., Laubacher, R. & Dellarocas, C. (2009). Harnessing crowds: Mapping the genome of collective intelligence. *Working Paper No. 2009-001*, Massachusetts Institute of Technology (MIT): Cambridge, 3 February.

McGonigal, J. (2011). *Reality is broken: Why games make us better and how they can change the world.* London: Random House.

Möslein, K. M., Haller, J. B. A., & Bullinger, A. C. (2010). Open evaluation: Ein IT-basierter ansatz für die bewertung innovativer konzepte, HMD sonderheft: *IT-basiertes Innovationsmanagement, 273,* 21–34.

Panksepp, J., & Burgdorf, J. (2003). 'Laughing' rats and the evolutionary antecedents of human joy? *Physiology & Behavior, 79*(3), 533–574.

Robra-Bissantz, S. & Lattemann, C. (2005). *Customer Integration and Customer Governance— Neue Konzepte für die Anbieter-Kunden-Beziehung im B2C-E-Business.* Paper presented at the Gemeinschaft in Neuen Medien (GeNeMe), 6–7 October, Dresden. http://www.uni-potsdam. de/db/jpcg/Publikationen/2005_9_GENEME_CI.pdf. Accessed 14 January 2016.

Reeves, B., & Read, J. L. (2009). *Total engagement: Using games and virtual worlds to change the way people work and businesses compete.* New York: McGraw-Hill Professional.

Salen, K., & Zimmerman, E. (2004). *Rules of play: Game design fundamentals.* Cambridge, Massachusetts: The MIT Press.

Scheiner, C. W. & Witt, M. (2012). *The longitudinal impact of game mechanics on motivation in the fuzzy front end.* European Academy of Management (EURAM): Rotterdam, Netherlands, 6 June–8 June.

Scheiner, C. W., Witt, M., Robra-Bissantz, S. & Voigt, K.-I. (2012). *Einsatz von Spielmechaniken in Ideenwettbewerben: Einsatzmotive, Wirkungen und Herausforderungen.* Paper presented at the Multikonferenz Wirtschaftsinformatik (MKWI), 29 February–2 March, Braunschweig, http://mkwi2012.de/downloads/MKWI2012_Tagungsband.pdf. Accessed 14 January 2016.

Schrage, M. (2000). *Serious play.* Cambridge: Harvard Business School Press.

Shneiderman, B. (1999). User interfaces for creativity support tools. In E. A. Edmonds, & Candy, L. (Eds.), *Proceedings of the Third Conference on Creativity and Cognition in Loughborough, England, 1999* (pp. 15–22). ACM Press: New York.

Spariosu, M. (1989). *Dionysis reborn: Play and the aesthetic dimension in modern philosophical and scientific discourse.* Ithaca: Cornell University Press.

Statler, M., Roos, J., & Victor, B. (2009). Ain't misbehavin': Taking play seriously in organizations. *Journal of Change Management, 9*(1), 87–101.

Takahashi, D. (2012). Game designers and rockefeller foundation attack poverty with fun. http:// venturebeat.com/2012/04/03/game-designers-and-rockefeller-foundation-attack-poverty-with-fun. Accessed 14 January 2016.

Witt, M., Scheiner, C. W., Robra-Bissantz, S. & Voigt, K.-I. (2012a). Creative process engagement in a multiplayer online ideation game. *Lecture Notes in Informatics (LNI) Proceedings,* P-208, (pp. 978–991).

Witt, M., Scheiner, C. W., Skornia, R., Robra-Bissantz, S. & Voigt, K.-I. (2011b). Wie Spielen komplexe Innovationsvorhaben unterstützt - Eine Fallstudienanalyse, *Beiträge zur wissenschaftlichen Konferenz "Innovation und Wettbewerb",* Sofia.

Zichermann, G., & Linder, J. (2010). *Game-based marketing: Inspire customer loyalty through rewards, challenges and contests.* New Jersey: Wiley.

Chapter 7
Social Collaboration and Gamification

**Christian Meske, Tobias Brockmann, Konstantin Wilms
and Stefan Stieglitz**

Abstract Despite the fact that enterprise social software solutions such as IBM Connections and Microsoft Sharepoint are able to increase the communication as well as the collaboration among employees, companies are constantly confronted with the necessity to improve their employees' motivation to interact with the system. Since gamification has been identified as an effective tool to enhance user acceptance, software developers adopt an increasing number of gamification elements to take advantage of it. Based on an in-depth analysis of the international market leaders in enterprise social software solutions, this chapter examines the implementation of gamification elements and critically reflects on how well they fit with the current insights of flow research in motivational psychology. We argue that current gamification elements predominately aim at the augmentation of the users' extrinsic motivation whereas intrinsic motivation has mostly been ignored. Furthermore, we identify a trend in which gamification solutions primarily focus on rewarding quantitative improvement of work activities, neglecting qualitative performance. Subsequently, current solutions do not match recent findings in research and ignore risks that can lower the employees' motivation and work performance in the long run.

7.1 Introduction

Due to the worldwide growing acceptance in societies, the concept of social media has increasingly shifted into organisations' focus of attention (Kane et al. 2014; Larosiliere et al. 2015). Nowadays digital platforms like Facebook, Twitter, LinkedIn, Google+, and YouTube are used for marketing activities or professional

C. Meske · K. Wilms · S. Stieglitz (✉)
Research Group Professional Communication in Electronic Media/Social Media,
Competence Center Connected Organization, Department of Computer Science
and Applied Cognitive Science, Innoscale AG, Berlin, Germany
e-mail: stefan.stieglitz@uni-due.de

T. Brockmann
Innoscale AG, Berlin, Germany

© Springer International Publishing Switzerland 2017
S. Stieglitz et al. (eds.), *Gamification*, Progress in IS,
DOI 10.1007/978-3-319-45557-0_7

communication such as political discussions (Chui et al. 2012; Kane et al. 2014; Stieglitz et al. 2014a). While the corporate usage of social media platforms for external communication, in order to deepen the relationships with consumers and business partners, has already reached a high level of recognition, the adoption of social media principles and functions within internal organisational structures is still a rising trend. These systems, namely social collaboration tools, (enterprise) social software or enterprise social media, are getting implemented to support communi-cation and collaboration among employees (Backhouse 2009). As those systems have the possibility to encourage the sharing of information and knowledge, and to support the internal communication independently from hierarchical structures, they can positively influence existing workflows and creativity processes (Chui et al. 2012; Meske et al. 2014). Organisations are confronted with the challenge of managing the adoption of such social collaboration tools and need to promote social software and find mechanisms to increase the employees' acceptance and usage (Stieglitz and Meske 2012; Meske and Stieglitz 2013). Pawlowski et al. (2014) identified in a structured literature review that the technical adoption and acceptance of technologies are some of the major issues hindering the use of social software.

One approach to improve the employees' acceptance, motivation and usage of software is gamification (Deterding et al. 2011). This approach is frequently examined in different professional fields (e.g., innovation management, knowledge sharing) by a multitude of researchers (Teh et al. 2013; Kaleta et al. 2014; Lounis et al. 2014). Gamification describes the application of typical game elements like high scores, badges, or virtual goods into traditional non-game contexts (e.g., learning, work). According to Stieglitz (2015) 'Enterprise Gamification' is defined as the integration of playful elements into business processes or into the learning environment of enterprises. Gamification works, as it makes use of basic human needs (e.g., success, reward, status, competition, self-expression, altruism) (Thiebes et al. 2014). Hence gamification helps to raise the extrinsic motivation of employees. However, although gamification has proven to be effective in the context of various information systems, this approach has also been criticised for diminishing users' motivation. For example Amriani et al. (2013) showed that elements like points, badges and leaderboards could diminish the intrinsic moti-vation of the users, since these elements only support extrinsic motivation. This effect of secondary extrinsic motivation lowering the primary intrinsic motivation is known as the 'overjustification effect' (deCharms 1968).

Enterprises, often start-ups, have begun to develop tools using gamification elements to enhance the benefits of social software. However, exemplary case studies have shown that current gamification technology only supports quantitative rather than qualitative work improvement (see e.g., Farzan et al. 2008; Amriani et al. 2013; Blohm and Leimeister 2013; De-Marcos et al. 2014), hence not con-sidering the above-described general criticism of gamification such as the over-justification effect. At the same time, the vendor market is in flux and an overview is still missing. This article therefore evaluates leading social software like IBM Connections, Jive or Microsoft SharePoint, regarding the support of gamification elements to shed light on the market. Besides the leading players, third party vendors offering gamification add-ons are considered for the market review. On this basis we critically reflect on how gamification is used in social software.

The remainder of the paper is structured as follows. First in Sect. 7.2 of this chapter the related scientific work about social collaboration software and their adoption is provided. The objective of this chapter is to clarify why projects of social collaboration projects often suffer from poor acceptance among the employees. In this context, gamification is introduced and described. Afterwards, the impact of using gamification mechanisms to support social collaboration is discussed. Based on this, in Sect. 7.3 a market review of gamification software for leading social collaboration tools is presented to show which technical capabilities are currently available. Afterwards the gamification functions are presented and critically discussed in Sect. 7.4. The article ends with a conclusion, summarising the key-findings of the critical review and providing advice for practitioners.

7.2 Literature Review and Theoretical Background

7.2.1 Social Collaboration

In literature, collaboration is described as the efforts of multiple individuals towards a mutually desired outcome (Briggs et al. 2006). Collaboration can be seen as a special type of process that includes communication, coordination and cooperation (Fan et al. 2012). In addition to this it is powerful for solving problems, making decisions and building consensus (Straus 2002). There is no need for employees to be physically present at the same place and time. Due to geographic or temporal reasons more and more people collaborate with each other via virtual technologies (Fan et al. 2012). One important aspect for providing a high level of collaboration performance is an enabling collaboration tool.

There are several theories that attempt to designate a set of principles for how to select the optimal tool for achieving the most successful collaboration process (Fan et al. 2012). *Task-Technology Fit Theory* (Zigurs et al. 1999) and *Media Richness Theory* (Daft and Lengel 1986) assert that the medium used for team communication needs to be well adapted to the type of information. *Process Virtualisation Theory* discusses the suitability of different processes to be conducted virtually. There are four cases which are less appropriate for virtualisation: human sensory experience, social context, time control and identity control (Fan et al. 2012). Schubert and Williams (2013) pointed out that one of the innovations in recent years was the application of the attribute '*social*' to the workplace. Companies increasingly pick up the concept of social media platforms like Facebook or Twitter and offer collaboration technology, which support employees' interaction and exchange of employee-generated content across the whole enterprise, possibly affecting formal aspects of the organisation including hierarchies and processes (Bögel et al. 2014; Stieglitz et al. 2014b; Riemer et al. 2015; Lattemann et al. 2009).

Collaboration technologies in general are 'computer-based applications that support selected groups or specialized teams that work in various industries to develop new knowledge' (Lamb and Dembla 2013, p. 94). Sarrel (2010) stated that document-centric traditional collaboration tools are not sufficient to drive innovation and productivity. It is rather important to be able to leverage voice, video, presence information and instant messaging. User profiles are also key components of social software. Workers can build their personal brand by creating their own profile, share content and experiences, find expertise and offer their own knowledge (Sarrel 2010). According to the McKinsey Global Institute report, two-thirds of the estimated economic value is due to improved communication and collaboration but a lot of companies are still missing a potentially 'huge prize'. Over 900 billion USD in annual value could be unlocked by products and services that facilitate social digital interactions. This is why enhancing the adoption of social collaboration technologies is an important process to manage.

One of the most highly cited models is the *Technology Acceptance Model*, which presents a way to measure the impact of external factors on internal beliefs, intentions and attitudes concerning user adoption of information systems (Davis 1985). According to this model external variables like pre-existing familiarity with social media can be useful so that users do not have to learn specific designs and applications within enterprise social software from scratch. These individual factors positively influence the perceived usefulness and ease of use. Other important aspects are the task complexity, organisational culture of the company and knowledge strategy. In the context of social software, collaboration can only proceed when the participants have the necessary trust in achieving the goal through the new system (Lawson et al. 2007). de Oliveira and Watson-Manheim (2013) asserted that the adoption and frequent usage of social software is not a controlled process but entails a dynamic process. Old and new processes can affect the adoption of social media tools, which may be 'constrained by existing processes but may also trigger creation of new ones' (De Oliveira and Watson-Manheim 2013, p. 2).

7.2.2 *Gamification*

An often cited definition in the literature describes gamification 'as the use of game elements and techniques in non-game contexts' (Deterding et al. 2011, p. 2). From the market service perspective gamification can be seen as 'the process of enhancing a service with affordances for gameful experiences in order to support user's overall value creation' (Huotari and Hamari 2012, p. 19). Zichermann and Cunningham (2011) considered gamification to be a process of game thinking that motivates users to perform particular tasks to solve problems or engage with customers. According to Shang and Lin (2013), games can be a powerful way to influence and change behaviour in any setting.

According to Zichermann, CEO of Gamification Co, the early adoptions of gamification occurred in response to employee dissatisfaction leading to disengagement. A recent Gallup poll revealed that two-thirds of the US workforce are disengaged or unengaged (Burmeister 2014). Yet, engagement of employees can create a 240 % increase of performance related outcomes. Especially for businesses that are facing generational workforce shifts, gamification could be useful (Burmeister 2014). Also Lounis et al. (2014) found that participants experienced more fun if they collaborated with others towards a common goal. Another positive aspect of collaboration in gamified information systems is the effect of 'social facilitation' which occurs when groups achieve better results than individuals (Zajonc 1965). Peischl et al. (2014) stated that gamification works as a layer on top of social collaboration software and Rampoldi-Hnilo and Snyder (2013) even considered mobile workers to be the perfect audience for gamified applications. This reveals that the phenomenon of gamification is increasingly integrated into information systems in the business context. However, the above-cited literature does not distinguish between incentive mechanisms to improve the quantity or quality of work, or relationships with others.

Gamification includes several game design elements like points, badges, leaderboards, rewards, levels, quests, challenges and virtual loops amongst others (Zichermann and Cunningham 2011; de Paoli et al. 2012; Domínguez et al. 2013). Those need to be implemented in the process of the transformation that incorporates game elements in the selected context. The motivation of using gamified elements lies in the satisfaction of fundamental human needs and desires, including the desire for reward, self-expression, altruism or competition (Bunchball Inc. 2010). In addition to this, the adequate combination of game mechanisms and dynamics should create a motivating, emotional and entertaining interaction (Neeli 2012). In this context, suitable systems have the potential to set the user into a state of 'flow' (Csikszentmihalyi 1991) where the user experiences a state of deep concentration. One of the conditions which must be fulfilled for a person to reach a state of flow is an adequate balance between challenge and skill. Therefore, in gamification environments, it is important for a task to match the user's skill level, where the user is neither under-challenged nor over-challenged (Groh 2012). Furthermore, gamified applications have to offer tasks in an interesting way, handing out 'juicy' feedback (Groh 2012). Flow Theory and its context in motivation psychology have been widely discussed in the current IS-literature. For an overview of the most common theoretical and methodical shortcomings see Mahnke (2014).

These motivating processes can be useful for adapting and using new or existing IS that otherwise often fail to meet their goals (Hsieh and Wang 2007). Especially intrinsic factors are important for motivating a certain behaviour (Deci and Ryan 2000). Intrinsic motivation means the process of doing something due to satisfaction from the activity itself while extrinsic motivation, in contrast, implies an activity due to the prospect of an external outcome (Deci and Ryan 2000). Shauchenka et al. (2014) pointed out that rewarding the quantitative performance of a user leads to a shift in motivation, where the user no longer enjoys the work itself but instead focuses on gaining points. According to the *Goal Contents Theory* (GCT) (Vansteenkiste et al. 2006) of *Self Determination Theory* (SDT) game elements that include monetary oriented goals can be seen as extrinsic stimuli whereas achievements to learn or improve in a certain activity lead to intrinsic motivation. While especially elements like points, badges, leaderboards and levels are used in the context of gamification design, it seems that those elements are not adequate to make gamification successful (Chorney 2012). While those elements may temporarily increase the performance of participating users (Mekler et al. 2013) it has been shown that the removal of those elements could interrupt user interaction on the provided system (Amriani et al. 2013). A reason for this might be that extrinsic rewards, punishments or regulations could diminish intrinsic motivations when individuals start to see the reward as the actual reason for performing an activity instead of doing so for their own interest or enjoyment (deCharms 1968; Cruz et al. 2015). This effect could be demonstrated in a simple experiment by Kohn (1999), where he showed that children getting paid for drawing pictures, produced more pictures, but of lesser quality. After the payment was interrupted, the children did not draw as much as they did before. In a situation where the quality of content is no longer taken into account, the user's interest might shift and as a consequence, the user may no longer be interested in contributing quality content (Shauchenka et al. 2014). Therefore the motivation shifts from intrinsic to extrinsic motivation and the user may get more motivated by gaining points, than by generating quality work (Shauchenka et al. 2014).

7.3 Market Review

7.3.1 Methodology

There are about 100 social software vendors on the market (Mladjov 2013). Considering all of them for this review would fall outside the scope of this article. First the number of social software vendors for the evaluation sample needs to be set. Analysts separate the market into four categories: (1) niche players, (2) visionaries, (3) challengers, and (4) leaders (Drakos et al. 2014). However, several approaches to differentiate the market in a first step exist and other business analyst may build on different samples. For the overriding goal of this paper—to conduct a critical market overview of gamification plug-ins for social software—the differentiation by Gartner Inc, a well-known market research institute. Their segmentation entails some restrictions as they only consider vendors who are active on at least three continents and have a turnover above $50 million. Hence, the goal of this article is to provide an overview of gamification functions from established social software and from third party vendors. Particularly the third party vendors merely concentrate their activities on leading platforms with high market share. Following Gartner these are software vendors, '*which have established their leadership through early recognition of users' needs, continuous innovation, significant market presence, and success in delivering user-friendly and solution focused suites with broad capabilities*' (Drakos et al. 2014). Based on the classification by Gartner, the five 'leading' vendors (IBM, Microsoft, Jive, Salesforce, Tibco

Software) comprised the unit for this analysis. The market examination was conducted in late 2014.

Next, the products of the vendors were selected. IBM, Jive and Tibco offer one social software product and were chosen for this market review. Microsoft and Salesforce offer more than one social software product. Microsoft offers SharePoint and Yammer as their social software products. Microsoft intends to concentrate their social activities on Yammer, but due to its long history, SharePoint is the leading product. Hence both products were considered in the market review. In addition, the products Chatter and Communities are offered by Salesforce. Communities concentrates on the support to establish large-scale communities of partners and customers, whereas Chatter is a tool for employee networking supporting collaboration features (Drakos et al. 2014). Due to the missing focus on collaboration, Communities was skipped and Chatter was selected for the sample.

In a next step the product websites of the software vendors were independently evaluated by two different researchers, regarding the availability of gamification functions. By doing so, several third party vendors offering plug-ins or add-ons for leading social software could be identified. However, not every social software vendor offered the necessary information on their website. Thus, a keyword-based web search was conducted. Table 7.1 shows the applied search strings used for the investigation via Google. The keywords were validated first by a pre-test and adjusted based on the first results during the search process. From the results page the first 10 results (1st page) were analysed. The method was used to gain first insights into the market. This approach resulted in an overview (Table 7.3) providing a short description and available gamification features (e.g., high scores, badges, and quests).

7.3.2   Results

Based on the search results derived by the keywords shown in Table 7.1, the two independent researchers were able to identify the third party vendors (plug-ins/add-ons) shown in Table 7.2. Both visited all websites generated by the Google search and manually created the vendor list. These third party vendors were selected for the market review regarding gamification features. The following sub-sections aim to briefly present the products and their main gamification functions.

7.3.2.1   Chatter

Salesforce Chatter does not contain any gamification functions, yet three third party plug-ins could be identified (Chatter answers, the Chatter game and RedCritter), which cover this domain. Using Chatter answers, the users gain points for certain activities within the network, particularly for answers. The peculiarity within this

Table 7.1 Search strings to identify third party vendors

Social software product (vendor)	Search strings to identify third party vendors (plug-ins and add-ons)
Chatter (Salesforce)	'chatter gamification' 'chatter gamification plugin' 'chatter gamification enterprise' 'chatter gamification standard'
IBM Connections (IBM)	'ibm connections gamification' 'ibm connections gamification plugin' 'ibm connections enterprise gamification' 'ibm connections gamification standard'
Sharepoint (Microsoft)	'sharepoint gamification' 'sharepoint gamification plugin' 'sharepoint gamification enterprise' 'sharepoint gamification standard'
tibbr (Tibco Software)	'tibbr gamification' 'tibbr gamification plugin' 'tibbr enterprise gamification' 'tibbr gamification standard'
JIVE (Jive)	'jive gamification' 'jive gamification plugin' 'jive gamification enterprise' 'jive gamification standard'
Yammer (Microsoft)	'yammer gamification' 'yammer gamification plugin' 'yammer enterprise gamification' 'yammer gamification standard'

Table 7.2 Overview of selected social software products and third party vendors

Social software product	Third party vendor
Chatter (Salesforce)	Chatter Answers The Chatter Game RedCritter
IBM Connections (IBM)	Kudos Badges Badgeville Nitro Bunchball
Sharepoint (Microsoft)	Badgeville Beezy RedCritter Attini
tibbr (Tibco Software)	(Announced partnership with) Badgeville
JIVE (JIVE)	Badgeville Nitro Bunchball
Yammer (Microsoft)	Face Game RedCritter Badgeville

tool is a live board that displays which user is the most active within the community in real time.

The Chatter game consists of posts that can be commented on by and within the community. This feedback affects the score, which is awarded for the post. The score is displayed, as well as the given feedback, in the user's personal profile. The prerequisite for this tool is an already active community. Also, this tool fosters an active community. When using RedCritter for Chatter, the users are engaged to earn rewards for activities, which they can share among the community members. This allows for a competition between the employees (see Sect. 7.3.2 of this chapter).

7.3.2.2 IBM Connections

Similar to Chatter (Salesforce), IBM does not offer any game mechanism within their collaboration software IBM Connections by default. To cover this domain, plug-ins are necessary. One plug-in is Kudos, which is based on reaching levels in different areas. In those different areas points are gained via activities so that new levels between 'Newbie' and 'Hall of Fame' might be reached. For each new level the employee gets a new badge, shown in the user's profile. Another feature is the 'thanks-function', which allows the user to give thanks to others for dispatching a task. This direct feedback by the co-workers motivates the users because they get a reward for their work. Another aspect is that the users can see how reliable another user is before they give him or her a task.

Another available plug-in is Nitro Bunchball. This plug-in allows the administrator to create different missions, which have to be accomplished by the users so that points and badges can be gained. Each mission is individually adjustable and there is the possibility of creating different blocks out of several missions. Furthermore the plug-in Badegeville allows the users to earn points and badges in two ways: either by active usage (sharing, participating in discussions) of the social-collaboration-tool (IBM Connections) or by fulfilling given missions, which contribute to a better acknowledgement of the tool. The level and badges, which are achieved by points, are shown in the user's profile and in the leaderboard.

7.3.2.3 SharePoint

SharePoint is the only social software product that offers gamification features by default. Since version 13.2 SharePoint contains two gamification features: first, the community template, which offers a discussion list based on various sites that are available for discussing. For each post points are gained and with a certain score badges for one's personal profile are achieved. Second, SharePoint provides an e-learning-feature. The users are gaining points as well as awards, which are shown in one's personal profile if they complete a so called class. E-learning classes can be online courses or classes, in which users can learn alone or together with a teacher and other employees. Besides these gamification features there are several third party plug-ins available. First, Badgeville offers the same features for SharePoint as for IBM Connections (see Sect. 7.2.2). The second one is RedCritter, which is also available for Chatter and Yammer. In sum, the employees get rewards in terms of points or badges for participation and further education. Those help the users to gain a higher level and can be reached via activities, both online as well as offline (e.g., via QR code). Both, levels and badges, are saved in the user's profile and can be seen by other staff in a leaderboard, which can be searched by special levels and badges by the team leaders.

Another plug-in by Beezy does not automatically reward the users, but the users mutually reward themselves. Beezy also offers the possibility of giving feedback, which is presented in one's personal profile. The last identified plug-in for SharePoint is Attini. Attini allows for gaining badges by certain social activities within SharePoint, which can be shown in one's personal profile.

7.3.2.4   tibbr

Tibco's tibbr does not include gamification features nor third party vendors offering gamification plug-ins or add-ons could be identified. However, in 2012 Tibco announced a partnership with Badgeville. It was intended to make it possible for tibbr users to earn contextually relevant rewards mapped to their expertise and contributions within the tibbr platform. So far it was not possible to identify any plug-in on the Badgeville or tibbr webpage.

7.3.2.5   Jive

The social software Jive does not contain any gamification functions yet. However, two third party plug-ins could be identified, enhancing the functionalities of Jive. The first one is Badgegeville and the second one is Nitro Bunchball. Both plug-ins are also available for IBM Connections and offer the same gamification features for both social software products. For more information see Sect. 7.2.2 of this chapter.

7.3.2.6   Yammer

Like the other social software products, except SharePoint, Yammer does not include any gamification features. However, there are third party plug-ins available, such as face game, a game in which the faces of other staff are shown and have to be recognised by the player. The users gain points for correct answers and are able to make comparisons with each other using a ranking. The idea behind this is that the team gets to know each other and the workers know who their teammates are, which can reduce the lack of communication and improve the working atmosphere.

The tool is suitable to integrate new members into a team or build up a new team. The already known plug-ins RedCritter and Badegeville are available for Yammer as well, with the gamification mechanisms described in Sects. 7.2.2 and 7.3.2 of this chapter.

7.4 Discussion

Summarising the market review (see Table 7.3) it can be stated that the market for gamification elements in social collaboration software is dominated by third party plug-ins. Only Microsoft SharePoint offers gamification features by default. One possible reason for this might be that due to the high quality of those plug-ins, the vendors of social collaboration tools may stop in-house development of gamification elements and cooperate with third party suppliers. According to the attributes and purposes of the plug-ins they can be divided into two categories.

The first category consists of tools, which seek to encourage the staff to improve their education. For accomplishing further development, points and rewards are provided, which portray a particular know-how of the user. Tools within this category are Kudos Badges, Face Game, RedCritter, and E-Learning-Function (SharePoint). The second category aims at the motivation of the staff to enhance their interaction within social collaboration software as well as motivating the employees to use the adapted tools actively and regularly. Therefore, this category does not aim to upgrade the staff's education but on the implementation of social collaboration tools in the workflow. The main aim is to create and motivate a community through social software. Solutions within this category are e.g. Attini, Nitro Bunchball, Chatter Answer, Chatter Game, and Community Template (SharePoint). Moreover, it could be observed that the third party vendors try to offer their services for a multitude of social software products. Especially Badgeville and RedCritter follow that approach. They put themselves in the position of gamification specialists for social software products and collaboration. Most of the offered gamification mechanisms are leaderboards, badges and points, while less often implemented mechanisms are challenges, quest, levels and rewards. Ownerships, bonus or status were not used in our sample.

While most of the third party vendors focused on reward mechanisms, none of the plug-ins took into account how to measure or reward qualitative performance. Most of the gamification plug-ins had a strong focus on rewarding quantitative user performance. Since points, badges and leaderboards have proven their influence in gamification systems by increasing users' participation and communication activity, the trend of adding those elements in social collaboration software seem to be legitimate. However, the 'efficiency' is quite questionable, since studies by Amriani et al. (2013) and Kohn (1999) indicated a possible overjustification effect, where users lose the intrinsic motivation in their work. Although different studies have shown that rewarding elements do not provide intrinsic motivation (Mekler et al. 2015), recent work indicated that rewarding elements could also be interpreted as

Table 7.3 Overview of applied game mechanisms

Social software	Third party vendors	Badges	Challenges/quests	Community collab.	Leaderboards	Levels	Points	Rewards/feedback
Chatter	Chatter Answers				x		x	
	The Chatter Game				x		x	
	RedCritter	x			x	x	x	x
IBM Connections	Kudos Badges	x		x	x		x	
	Badgeville	x	x		x	x	x	
	Nitro Bunchball	x	x		x	x	x	
SharePoint	Badgeville	x	x		x	x	x	
	Beezy	x						x
	RedCritter	x			x	x	x	x
	Attini	x						
SP: Community Template		x			x		x	
SP: E-Learning Feature					x		x	
tibbr	Not available							
Jive	Badgeville	x	x		x	x	x	
	Nitro Bunchball	x	x		x	x	x	
Yammer	Face Game				x		x	
	RedCritter	x			x	x	x	x
	Badgeville	x	x		x	x	x	

intrinsic motivators in a gaming context (Cruz et al. 2015). Even if the gaming context seems not to be the same as social software environments, these findings are interesting and fit the taxonomy of human motivation by Deci and Ryan (2000). The taxonomy of human motivation describes the effect where extrinsic motivation leads to intrinsic motivation over time. Both the findings by Cruz et al. 2015 and the findings of Deci and Ryan (2000) need to be researched in the context gamification in social software. Nevertheless, there is still a rather one-sided view on rewarding quantitative performance, which is also criticised in studies by Schubert et al. (2014) and Shauchenka et al. (2014). Therefore, in future research the long-term effectiveness of such systems has to be investigated and discussed in more detail. It seems that the trend of current gamification implementations mainly focuses on increasing quantitative performance in the first IT-adoption phase and that long-term goals are missing. It seems that the goal of placing users into a state of 'flow' has not been sufficiently considered yet.

7.5   Conclusion

The benefits of collaboration software in organisational environments as well as the tremendous diffusion of tools have been well documented in prior work. Organisations are faced with managing the adoption of these collaborative tools and therefore need to increase the acceptance and usage motivation. One way to solve this problem can be gamification. As prior work has shown, gamification elements in social software are able to improve user's engagement through extrinsic motivation and therefore lead to a better acceptance of the system. However, while gamification has been adequately discussed in the literature, the market for collaborative software is still young and fluctuating. Research has ignored several market determining tools as well as third party vendor solutions. Consequently an overview of major collaboration tools and the possibilities to use the tools in a gamified way were missing. In this work we tried to fill this gap by analysing major social software solutions as well as third party vendors offering gamification add-ons to those. We found that while social software tools primarily do not include gamification elements, plenty of third party vendors offer add-ons to embed gamification elements to the software. In addition we made several research contributions and highlighted that current gamification approaches often ignores findings of scientists: although the simple usage of purely extrinsic motivators entails the risk of lowering a user's intrinsic motivation and causing a dismissal of the system or even the work task in the long run, gamification features still focus on exactly those mechanisms. Most notably, promoting intrinsic motivation has been mainly neglected in the implementations. The aim in current implementations is often to increase the quantitative performance instead of the qualitative performance. Since the user gets rewarded for doing nothing but quantitative work, according to Groh (2012) a state of flow cannot be reached. Overall, our findings showed a gap between current research and practical usage.

Our work focused on collaboration software with high market shares, and we were only able to analyse a small group of tools and third party vendors. In any case, the issue of different gamification types deserve future research attention in the context of gamification of collaborative environments. Implementations also need to support the emergence of intrinsic motivation. Research should support development by identifying new strategies and gamification elements that match the corresponding requirements.

Acknowledgments This contribution is an updated and edited version of the conference article: Meske et al. (2015).

References

Amriani, A., Aji, A. F., Utomo, A. Y., & Junus, K. M. (2013). An empirical study of gamification impact on e-learning environment. In *Proceedings of 2013 3rd International Conference on Computer Science and Network Technology, IEEE* (pp. 265–269).

Backhouse, J. (2009) Social media: Impacting the enterprise?. In *European and Mediterranean Conference on Information Systems* (pp. 1–9).

Blohm, I., & Leimeister, J. M. (2013). Gamification: Design of IT-based enhancing services for motivational support and behavioral change. *Business and Information Systems Engineering, 5* (4), 275–278.

Bögel, S., Stieglitz, S., & Meske, C. (2014). A role model-based approach for modelling collaborative processes. *Business Process Management Journal (BPMJ), 20*(4), 598–614.

Briggs, R., Kolfschoten, G., Gert-Jan, V., & Douglas, D. (2006). Defining key concepts for collaboration engineering. In *AMCIS 2006 Proceedings* (p. 17).

Bunchball Inc. (2010). Gamification 101: An introduction to the use of game dynamics to influence behavior. http://www.bunchball.com/sites/default/files/downloads/gamification101.pdf. Accessed December 9, 2015.

Burmeister, B. (2014). Befriend the trend—Gaming goes to work. *Finweek*, p. 7.

Chorney, A. I. (2012). Taking the game out of gamification. *Dalhousie Journal of Interdisciplinary Management, 8*(1), 1–14.

Chui, M., Manyika, J., Bughin, J., Dobbs, R., Roxburgh, C., Sarrazin, H., Sands, G., & Westergren, M. (2012). The social economy: Unlocking value and productivity through social technologies. *McKinsey Global Institute*, 1–18.

Cruz, C., Hanus, M. D., & Fox, J. (2015). The need to achieve: Players' perceptions and uses of extrinsic meta-game reward systems for video game consoles. *Computers in Human Behavior*.

Csikszentmihalyi, M. (1991). *Flow: The psychology of optimal experience (41)*. New York: Harper Perennial.

Daft, R. L., & Lengel, R. H. (1986). Organizational information requirements, media richness and structural design. *Management Science, 32*(5), 554–571.

Davis, F. D. (1985). A technology acceptance model for empirically testing new end-user information systems: theory and results. *Massachusetts Institute of Technology*.

deCharms, R. (1968). Personal causation. *Journal of Applied Social Psychology, 2*(2), 95–113.

de Oliveira, G. H. M., & Watson-Manheim, M. B. (2013). Use of social media in the workplace: Contradictions and unintended consequences. In *19th Americas Conference on Information Systems, Chicago, Illinois* (pp. 1–8).

de Paoli, S., De Uffici, N., & D'Andrea, V. (2012). Designing badges for a civic media platform: Reputation and named levels. In *Proceedings of the 26th annual BCS interaction specialist group conference on people and computers* (pp. 59–68), British Computer Society.

De-Marcos, L., Domínguez, A., Saenz-De-Navarrete, J., & Pagés, C. (2014). An empirical study comparing gamification and social networking on e-learning. *Computers & Education, 75*, 82–91.

Deci, E. L., & Ryan, R. M. (2000). The 'what' and 'why' of goal pursuits: Human needs and the self-determination of behavior. *Psychological Inquiry, 11*(4), 227–268.

Deterding, S., Dixon, D., Khaled, R., & Nacke, L. (2011). From game design elements to gamefulness. In *Proceedings of the 15th International Academic MindTrek Conference on Envisioning Future Media Environments—MindTrek'11* (pp. 9–15). New York, USA: ACM Press.

Domínguez, A., Saenz-De-Navarrete, J., De-Marcos, L., Fernández-Sanz, L., Pagés, C., & Martínez-Herráiz, J. J. (2013). Gamifying learning experiences: Practical implications and outcomes. *Computers & Education, 63*, 380–392.

Drakos, N., Mann, J., Rozwell, C., Austin, T., & Sarner, A. (2014). Magic quadrant for social software in the workplace. *Gartner Inc.*, https://www.gartner.com/doc/2836617/magic-quadrant-social-software-workplace. Accessed December 9, 2015.

Fan, S., Sia, C., L., & Zhai, J. L., (2012). Towards collaboration virtualization theory. In *PACIS 2012 Proceedings* (p 5).

Farzan, R., DiMicco, J. M., Millen, D. R., Dugan, C., Geyer, W., & Brownholtz, E. A. (2008). Results from deploying a participation incentive mechanism within the enterprise. In: *Proceeding of the twenty-sixth annual CHI conference on Human factors in computing systems —CHI'08* (p. 563). New York, USA: ACM Press.

Groh, F. (2012). Gamification: State of the art definition and utilization. *Research Trends in Media Informatics, 4*, 39–46.

Hsieh, J. J. P.-A., & Wang, W. (2007). Explaining employees' extended use of complex information systems. *European Journal of Information Systems, 16*, 216–227.

Huotari, K., & Hamari, J. (2012). Defining gamification. In *Proceeding of the 16th International Academic Conference on MindTrek—MindTrek'12* (p. 17). New York, USA: ACM Press.

Kaleta, J. P., Kettinger, W. J., & Zhang, C. (2014). Achieving business goals with gamification: An informational and motivational perspective. In *20th Americas Conference on Information Systems* (Vol. 3, p. 2455).

Kane, G. C., Palmer, D., Phillips, A. N., & Kiron, D. (2014). Finding the value in social media data. *MIT Sloan Management Review*.

Kohn, A. (1999). *Punished by rewards: The problem with gold stars, A's, praise, and other bribes*. Boston: Houghton Mifflin Harcourt.

Lamb, L., & Dembla, P. (2013). Development of a research model to improve performance outcomes using collaboration technologies. In *SAIS 2013 Proceedings* (Vol. 16, p. 19).

Larosiliere, G., Meske, C., & Carter, L. (2015). Determinants of social network adoption: A country-level analysis. In *Proceedings of the 48th Hawaii International Conference on System Sciences (HICSS)* (pp. 3424–3433).

Lattemann, C., Stieglitz, S., & Kupke, S. (2009). Deutsche Unternehmen auf dem Weg zum Web 2.0?. HMD-Praxis der. *Wirtschaftsinformatik, 46*(3), 18–26.

Lawson, R., Hol, A., & Hall, T. (2007). Challenges of eCollaboration among SMEs. In *20th Bled eConference eMergence: Merging and Emerging Technologies, Processes, and Institutions* (pp. 648–660).

Lounis, S., Pramatari, K., & Theotokis, A. (2014). Gamification is all about fun: The role of incentive type and community collaboration. In *ECIS 2014 Proceedings* (Vol. 22, Track 12, Paper 13).

Mahnke, R., Benlian, A., & Hess, T. (2014). Flow experience in information systems research: Revisiting its conceptualization, conditions, and effects.

Mekler, E. D., Brühlmann, F., Opwis, K., & Tuch, A. N. (2013). Do points, levels and leaderboards harm intrinsic motivation?. In *Proceedings of the First International Conference on Gameful Design, Research, and Applications—Gamification'13* (pp. 66–73).

Mekler, E. D., Brühlmann, F., Tuch, A. N., & Opwis, K. (2015). Towards understanding the effects of individual gamification elements on intrinsic motivation and performance. In *Computers in Human Behavior*.

Meske, C., Brockmann, T., Wilms, K., & Stieglitz, S. (2015). Gamify employee collaboration—A critical review of gamification elements in social software. In *Proceedings of the 26th Australasian Conference on Information Systems (ACIS)*.

Meske, C., & Stieglitz, S. (2013). Adoption and use of social media in small and medium-sized enterprises. In *Proceedings of the 6th Practice-Driven Research on Enterprise Transformation* (pp. 61–75). Lecture Notes in Business Information Processing (LNBIP).

Meske, C., Stieglitz, S., & Middelbeck, D. (2014). Mehrwerte von intranet social software—Status quo in der Wissenschaft. *Tagungsband der Multikonferenz Wirtschaftsinformatik (MKWI), 2014*, 1775–1785.

Mladjov, V. (2013). List of enterprise social collaboration companies. http://blogs.gartner.com/vassil-mladjov/list-of-enterprise-social-collaboration-companies/. Accessed December 9, 2015.

Neeli, B. K. (2012). A method to engage employees using gamification in BPO Industry. In *3rd International Conference on Services in Emerging Markets* (pp. 142–146).

Pawlowski, J. M., Bick, M., Martensen, M., Peinl, R., Thalmann, S., Maier, R., et al. (2014). Social knowledge environments. *Business and Information Systems Engineering, 6*(2), 81–88.

Peischl, B., Schantl, J., & Holzinger, A. (2014). Energizing people's work: Transforming organizations through gamification. In A. Butz, M. Koch, & J. Schlichter (Eds.), *Tagungsband der Konferenz Mensch & Computer* (pp. 3–14).

Rampoldi-Hnilo, L., & Snyder, M. (2013). The business love triangle-smartphones, gamification, and social collaboration. *Lecture Notes in Computer Science (including subseries Lecture Notes in Artificial Intelligence and Lecture Notes in Bioinformatics)* (Vol. 8005 LNCS, pp. 309–315).

Riemer, K., Stieglitz, S., & Meske, C. (2015). From top to bottom: Investigating the changing role of hierarchy in enterprise social networks. *Business Information Systems Engineering (BISE), 57*(3), 197–212.

Sarrel, M. (2010). Tapping the positive from social networks for collaboration. *eWeek, 27*, 22–26.

Schubert, P., Paulsen, L., & Hager, J. (2014). Auswirkungen von gamification in enterprise collaboration systems. *Tagungsband der Konferenz Mensch & Computer*, 1–12.

Schubert, P., & Williams, S. P. (2013). The concept of social business: Oxymoron or sign of a changing work culture? In *BLED 2013 Proceedings* (pp. 222–235).

Shang, S. S. C., & Lin, K. Y. (2013). An understanding of the impact of gamification on purchase intentions. In *Proceedings of the Nineteenth Americas Conference on Information Systems* (pp. 1–11).

Shauchenka, N., Ternès, A., & Towers, I. (2014). In G. A. Ternès & I. Towers (Eds.), *Internationale Trends in der Markenkommunikation - Was Globalisierung, neue Medien und Nachhaltigkeit erfordern* (pp. 33–50).

Stieglitz, S. (2015). Gamification – Vorgehen und Anwendung. *HMD Praxis der Wirtschaftsinformatik*, 1–10. Online First, doi:10.1365/s40702-015-0185-6

Stieglitz, S., Dang-Xuan, L., Bruns, A., & Neuberger, C. (2014a). Social media analytics: An interdisciplinary approach and its implications for information systems. *Business and Information Systems Engineering (BISE), 6*(2), 89–96.

Stieglitz, S., & Meske, C. (2012). Maßnahmen für die Einführung und den Betrieb unternehmensinterner Social Media. *HMD-Praxis der Wirtschaftsinformatik, 52*(6), 816–825.

Stieglitz, S., Riemer, K., & Meske, C. (2014b). Hierarchy or activity? The role of formal and informal influence in eliciting responses from enterprise social networks. In *Proceedings of the 22nd European Conference on Information Systems (ECIS)* (Track 07, Paper 12).

Straus, D. (2002). *How to make collaboration work: Powerful ways to build consensus, solve problems, and make decisions*. San Francisco: Berrett-Koehler Publishers.

Teh, N., Schuff, D., Johnson, S., & Geddes, D. (2013). Can work be fun? Improving task motivation and help-seeking through game mechanics. *International Conference on Information Systems (ICIS 2013): Reshaping Society Through Information Systems Design, 2013* (Vol. 1, pp. 680–687).

Thiebes, S., Lins, S., & Basten, D. (2014). Gamifying information systems—A synthesis of gamification mechanics and dynamics. In *Proceedings of the 22nd European Conference on Information Systems (ECIS)* (Track 01, Paper 04).

Vansteenkiste, M., Lens, W., & Deci, E. L. (2006). Intrinsic versus extrinsic goal contents in self-determination theory: Another look at the quality of academic motivation. *Educational Psychologist, 41*(1), 19–31.

Zajonc, R. B. (1965). Social Facilitation. *Science, 149*(3681), 269–274.

Zichermann, G., & Cunningham, C. (2011). *Gamification by design: Implementing game mechanics in web and mobile apps Oreilly & Associates Inc.* Sebastopol: O'Reilly Media.

Zigurs, I., Buckland, B. K., Connolly, J. R., & Wilson, E. V. (1999). A test of task-technology fit theory for group support systems. *ACM SIGMIS Database, 30*(3–4), 34–50.

Chapter 8
A Serious Game as a Market Research Method for Purchase Decision Processes

Silke Plennert

Abstract Over the past few years games, and gamification have become increasingly widespread in numerous business sectors. The serious game introduced in this chapter is designed as a qualitative market research method, thereby showing a comparatively new field of application for games. It can be used in place of classical qualitative methods, such as focus groups or interviews. It reduces the weaknesses of such techniques, whilst simultaneously using the advantages of game thinking. The game maps the information search during a purchase decision process and enables the probands to play their individual information search process. During this procedure, they reveal valuable insights into their needs. These insights could help organisations to influence their customers at the relevant touch points during the decision process.

8.1 Introduction

Game thinking—the 'process of addressing problems like a game designer, by looking at how to motivate players and create engaging fun experiences' (Werbach and Hunter 2012, p. 131)—has become a major trend in recent years. There are countless academic studies proving the positive effects of game thinking (e.g., increased motivation or endurance) in many different areas, for example e-learning (Cheong et al. 2013), innovation management (Witt et al. 2011), and medical science (Halan et al. 2010).

Nevertheless, there are still industries for which game thinking is a comparatively new concept. In this chapter we examine a serious game that has been developed as a new qualitative market research method. The game enables probands to play the purchase decision process—or more precisely the information

S. Plennert (✉)
Institut für Wirtschaftsinformatik, Technische Universität Braunschweig,
Braunschweig, Germany
e-mail: s.plennert@tu-braunschweig.de

© Springer International Publishing Switzerland 2017
S. Stieglitz et al. (eds.), *Gamification*, Progress in IS,
DOI 10.1007/978-3-319-45557-0_8

search—of a customer purchasing a car. The incorporated game design elements help to gain relevant customer insights.

First, a brief look at purchase decision processes shows the relevance of knowing one's customers' information needs. This is followed by a summary of current market research methods and their deficits. The term *serious game* is subsequently distinguished from adjacent areas in the game thinking domain. Furthermore, the potential benefits for market research achieved through the use of games are examined. The following sections describe the serious game that has been developed and its application as a market research method. The final section provides a brief conclusion.

8.2   Gaining Insights into the Purchase Decision Process

8.2.1   Relevance of Information Needs

Purchase decision processes are becoming more and more complex from the perspective of companies, and thus less comprehensible. One major reason is the growing influence of digital touch points on the relationship between companies and their customers (TNS Infratest 2010; Munzinger and Wenhart 2012). On the one hand, the percentage of online purchases is increasing (Heinemann 2012), and on the other hand, purchase decision processes take place increasingly in the digital world (Heinemann 2013).

During this process, the customers have information needs that must be fulfilled. They seek certain answers and want to reduce uncertainty to be able to come to a decision (Case 2012). In order to completely understand their customers and hence be able to connect to and support them (e.g., by introducing e-services), companies must gain better insights into these information needs.

8.2.2   Market Research Methods

There are several methods currently in use for gaining customer insights into various aspects of the purchase process. In general, the use of classical qualitative market research methods is most common, especially focus groups, as well as various forms of qualitative interviews. Additionally, more methods are being adapted or even developed specifically for investigating the purchase decision process. Examples of process accompanying approaches are diary studies (van Douwe 2011).

These methods have exhibited a variety of problems. In addition to the general issue of motivating those participating in studies, several scientists have acknowledged the fact that insights into purchase processes still cannot be gathered to a sufficient degree. The methods employed are outdated and provide only hypothetical and unrealistic results (Belz et al. 2011). Probands are rarely able to describe their purchase decision retrospectively, since it is mainly an emotional process (Wellner 2003). With process accompanying methods, the issue of identifying and acquiring relevant test participants is problematic. Additionally, the studies run the risk of influencing the decision process (van Douwe 2011). Another weakness that applies especially to focus groups and interviews is the significant impact of the moderator and other participants. The situation can lead to false (e.g., socially desirable) responses, since the test persons are aware of being interviewed the whole time (Boateng 2012).

These and further obstacles lead to the conclusion that it is necessary to develop new market research methods for gaining insights into the purchase decision process. The next section introduces serious games and their potential for market research.

8.3 Serious Games

8.3.1 Definition und Classification

The game thinking domain consists of two major research fields: *serious games* and *gamification*. Deterding et al. (2011a, b) developed a graphical presentation that differentiates *gamification* and *games*, as well as *toys* and *playful design*, along two axes (see Fig. 8.1).

The vertical axis shows a continuum between playing and gaming—the latter meaning that some kind of game design is being applied. The horizontal axis depicts the difference between designing a full game and merely employing some game elements in other contexts.

Fig. 8.1 Serious games and related research fields. Adapted from Deterding et al. (2011a, b)

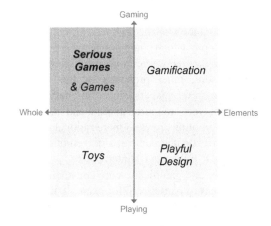

Gamification, games and serious games are located in the top half of the matrix, since they all include the application of game design. According to a widely recognised definition, gamification can be described as 'the use of game design elements in non-game contexts' (Deterding et al. 2011b, p. 2).

Games are placed in the top left corner—differentiating them from sole game elements or play without a game design. There are many different definitions for the term game. An overview and comparison are given by Salen and Zimmerman (2004). One of these definitions comes from Clark Abt. He stated that 'a game is an activity among two or more independent decision-makers seeking to achieve their objectives in some limiting context' (Abt 1987, p. 6). Later on, a game has been defined as 'a problem-solving activity, approached with a playful attitude' (Schell 2008). These two definitions seem most suitable for the analysed background, since the two activities decision-making and problem-solving are in line with the purchase decision process.

Serious games are also games, but with another purpose than mere entertainment, for example teaching the player something (Abt 1987). Sawyer and Smith (2008) demonstrated that serious games now cover a wider range of goals and classified them according to seven categories, one of which is named *Games for Science and Research*. The serious game examined in the following can be placed in this category.

8.3.2 Improving Market Research with Serious Games

Playing games has several impacts on the players. Possible effects of using games or game design elements include increased creativity and motivation of the player, and the achievement of a so-called flow state. These results have been shown in a variety of scientific studies—see for example Berlyne (1969), Chen (2007), Csikszentmihalyi (1990), and Witt and Robra-Bissantz (2012).

In addition to these general effects, games have advantages over other methods that are especially interesting for market researchers. They allow the players (who in this context are also the probands or test participants) to immerse themselves deeply into the topic, which could not be achieved otherwise. As a result, the players get in a so-called flow and give more valid answers (Füller and Hutter 2012; Janke 2012). Furthermore, other probands or the interviewers/moderators exert less of an influence on the players, since the interview situation fades into the background.

The players are more attentive and also more authentic, as the game allows them to show emotions beyond mere rational aspects. This leads to a more realistic view of the investigated subject, since emotions are often crucial in decision processes (Abt 1987; Füller and Hutter 2012).

Games and gamification are considered more fun and there is therefore a higher willingness to participate (for example in market research experiments) as well as a lower dropout rate (for example when filling out questionnaires). This also leads to better results, since the players do not lose interest or concentration during the interview or focus group session (Singer et al. 1999; MacElroy and Gray 2003; Füller and Hutter 2012; Janke 2012).

Based on these findings, a serious game has been developed to use as a market research method for gaining insights into purchase decision processes. Section 8.4 of this chapter introduces the game, before its use as a market research method is described in Sect. 8.5 of this chapter.

8.4   The Game

8.4.1   Overview

The serious game that has been developed simulates the information search during a purchase decision process. The purchase of a new car was chosen as a concrete application because of its extensive decision process. An extensive decision process is typically very comprehensive and time-consuming. The customers have a high involvement and purchase motivation, while there is also a great purchase risk (Diller 2007). Therefore, insights into the customers' information needs are especially relevant.

The serious game consists of a board game combined with a smartphone application. From the players' point of view, the goal is to be the first to park their car in the middle of the board after having reached a predefined number of *information fields*. These fields represent the different touch points between the customer and a product or brand during the decision process, such as the company's website, conversations with friends about that product, or direct contact with it.

Figure 8.2 shows the game board. The players start in the corners and move their cars on the roads, trying to approach the information fields.

Figure 8.3 shows two screenshots of the mobile application. Every time the players arrive at an information field, they can push one of the three round buttons in the app (left screen) and answer the questions that consequently appear (right screen). The dialog shown in the right screen is split into three parts. The first one is the information source category the player previously chose for seeking information. Here, he or she can select from the Internet, personal conversations, direct experience and advertising. In the second part, the player has to write down the precise source he or she would refer to when deciding what car to purchase. The last part asks for the detailed information or service the player is looking for within that source. To name an example, a player could choose *Internet* and state that she would ask her friends on Facebook about positive driving experiences with different cars at high speed.

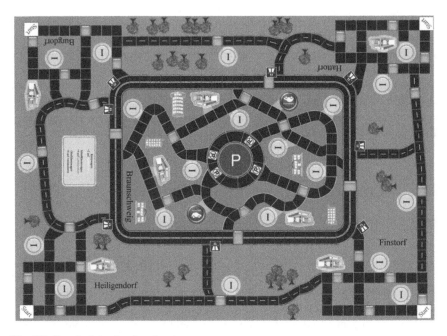

Fig. 8.2 Board of the developed serious game

Fig. 8.3 Screenshots of the serious game's mobile application

8.4.2 Game Design Elements

The game has been designed and developed according to certain game design guidelines (Salen and Zimmerman 2004; Schell 2008). Schell defined that a game consists of many different elements, which can be sorted into four basic categories: *story*, *mechanics*, *aesthetics* and *technology*. Every game needs to have elements from all categories. They influence each other and together they determine the player experience (Schell 2008). Below, a brief overview of the applied game design elements is given. For details about the game and more information about the theoretical background see Plennert and Robra-Bissantz (2014).

The story of a game needs to have at least the following two aspects: a goal the player has to reach and obstacles on the journey to that goal, which can lead to interesting conflicts between the players (Schell 2008). The main goal for the players in this game is to reach a certain amount of information fields—representing different touch points during their purchase decision process—and to park their car. Various game elements can provide obstacles, e.g. some cards allow players to interfere with each other. Game mechanics are defined as all procedures and interactions during the game, with objects and rules being of capital importance (Schell 2008). In this case, examples of objects include the dice, tokens or cards, regardless of whether they exist as tangible objects or virtual objects on the smartphone app. The aesthetics of a game are important for the look and feel, and can therefore help to make the story come to life (Schell 2008). The design of the game board and the GUI of the app are examples of this category. Technology describes all the tools and materials that are used to create the game, especially the game aesthetics. It can range from paper and pencil to a computer programme (Schell 2008). The technology in this game lies mainly in the design of the game board and parts of the app with Adobe Photoshop, as well as the development of the smartphone application with Android Studio.

8.5 The Game as a Market Research Method

8.5.1 Using the Game

The purpose of the game is to gain valuable insights into the information needs customers have during the purchase decision process of buying a new car. This includes their preferred information sources and the touch points they are influenced by, and their motives for using a particular source for specific information.

Research institutes, market research agencies, market research departments of car companies and car dealers could provide the game. The target group depends mainly on the researchers and what they want to discover. Car companies could use the results in numerous ways, for example to satisfy their potential customers at the relevant touch points, and thereby increase customer loyalty.

The game is conducted in a laboratory environment where up to four players can be invited to a play session. A moderator explains the basic rules and stays in the vicinity so they can step in if questions or problems occur. He or she also prompts the probands to *think aloud* during the whole game—a popular method used 'to gain insight in the knowledge and methods of human problem-solving' (van Someren et al. 1994, pp. 1–2). In addition to the notes that the researchers can take during the session, the players are taped.

8.5.2 Gaining Insights with the Game

Insights are generated directly and indirectly. The direct way includes the above-mentioned setting and the information the probands reveal whilst playing the game. Before playing the game, the participants choose a car (from a given list), pick their preferred information source categories and sort them according to their importance in their personal decision process. During the game, the players talk about certain aspects of their information needs and type them into the app. In addition, the other players can make inquiries about or agree with these statements. Most of what happens in the app can be transmitted in real-time to the researcher.

The applied game design elements indirectly support the insight generating process. On the one hand, a positive player experience is achieved through the interaction and balance of the story, mechanics, aesthetics and technology. This makes the game fun and players are therefore more motivated to participate. On the other hand, several of the applied elements lead to a high level of immersion in the game world and, in turn, in the situation of real decision-making. These elements include the task of driving to different information fields or certain cards. Event cards, which are frequently drawn throughout the game, stimulate the players to think about their needs by addressing different situations throughout the decision process. For example, one card forces a player to miss a turn because they did not take a test drive before buying their car, so they still need to get used to it. The individual *goal card* that each player draws at the beginning of the game encourages discussions. The card describes a secret mission the player has to fulfil, for example to challenge their left neighbour's statements by giving counterexamples from their personal experience. All together, the game design elements mean that the game experience becomes more vital to the players than the interview situation. They stay interested and focussed throughout the whole play session. They can show emotions, be authentic and reveal better insights as they not only talk about the decision process, but re-enact it. Therefore the answers they give are more honest and more realistic than with other research methods. These indirect ways of gaining insights are drawn from the findings described in Sect. 8.3.2 of this chapter.

Figure 8.4 summarises the different ways in which insights into the players' information needs are generated, both directly and indirectly.

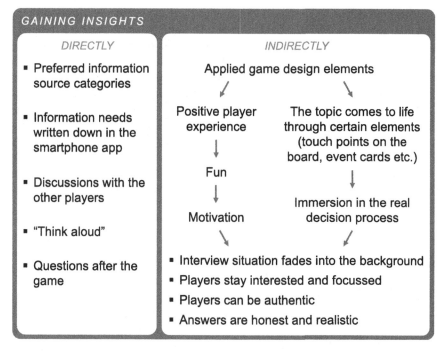

Fig. 8.4 Gaining insights into information needs within the game

8.5.3 Testing the Game

A major part of the game design process is the so-called *playtesting* (Fullerton 2008; Schell 2008). The goal is to improve the game as much as possible, so that it creates a positive experience for the players and eventually results in the effects shown in Fig. 8.4. Each playtest leads to improvements that are implemented immediately, so that the next playtest is conducted with an enhanced version of the game.

As mentioned above, the game is executed in a laboratory environment. The playtests have been conducted in a secluded room at the university, where the players sat at a table with the game board and were provided with smartphones, rules and other necessary items. In the first phase, the game designers and developers (a research team consisting of one research assistant and five students) acted as the playtesters and took part in many playtests. In the second phase, probands were recruited at the university (in this phase they were solely students). In addition to the research team, there were 37 tissue-testers, i.e. they participated only once in the game and had no prior knowledge of it. There were 27 male and 10 female players, between the ages of 20–29. At the beginning of each playtest, the moderator (a member of the research team) gave a short introduction, started the audiotaping, and then stayed in the background.

After the playtest, the probands filled out an individual questionnaire and took part in a group discussion about the game. The questionnaire included questions about the game itself and the smartphone application. To give two examples, most players had fun playing the game and thought that the app supported the game process. Test results also demonstrated that probands were very open-minded about the new method and discussed their information needs freely. In addition to the insights revealed during the play sessions, most probands were keen to join in further discussions afterwards.

In the next phase, the game as a market research method will be evaluated during an experiment. The game and a form of the qualitative interview will be carried out so the results can be compared. Probands will be recruited at a car company and at the university (students as well as research assistants), and they will be assigned randomly to the two methods.

8.6 Conclusion

Games and gamification are becoming more and more widespread throughout the business world. However, the serious game presented here shows a relatively new area of application for games. The game is designed as a new market research method—an alternative to current methods like focus groups or interviews. By using it, one can gain insights into the information needs of car buyers during their purchase decision process. The method takes the advantages of game thinking and transfers them to market research. As a result, several weaknesses of the known methods are reduced, for example the problem of unrealistic answers when analysing processes.

In summary, it can be stated that the new method has a high potential to deliver better results than current methods. The game is currently only designed for the purchase of cars, but by changing a few game design elements, it could be adapted to other products or to simulate different processes altogether.

References

Abt, C. C. (1987). *Serious games*. Lanham: University Press of America.
Belz, C., Huber, D., Okonek, C., & Rutschmann, M. (2011). Reales Kundenverhalten—Reales marketing. In C. Belz (Ed.), *Innovationen im Kundendialog* (pp. 107–123). Wiesbaden: Gabler.
Berlyne, D. E. (1969). Laughter, humor, and play. In G. Lindzey & E. Aronson (Eds.), *The handbook of social psychology* (pp. 795–852). Reading: Addison-Wesley.
Boateng, W. (2012). Evaluating the efficacy of focus group discussion (FGD) in qualitative social research. *International Journal of Business & Social Science, 3*(7), 54–57.
Case, D. O. (2012). *Looking for information: A survey of research on information seeking, needs, and behavior* (3rd ed.). Bingley, UK: Emerald Group Pub.
Chen, J. (2007). Flow in games (and everything else). *Communications of the ACM, 50*(4), 31–34.

Cheong, C., Cheong, F., & Filippou, J. (2013). Quick quiz: A gamified approach for enhancing learning. In *PACIS 2013 Proceedings*, Paper 206.

Csikszentmihalyi, M. (1990). *Flow: The psychology of optimal experience*. New York: HarperCollins.

Deterding, S., Dixon, D., Khaled, R., & Nacke, L. E. (2011a). From game design elements to gamefulness: Defining "Gamification." In *Proceedings of the 15th International Academic MindTrek Conference: Envisioning Future Media Environments* (pp. 9–15).

Deterding, S., Khaled, R., Nacke, L. E., & Dixon, D. (2011b). Gamification: Toward a definition. In *CHI 2011 Gamification Workshop Proceedings* (pp. 6–9).

Diller, H. (2007). *Grundprinzipien des Marketing* (2nd ed.). Nürnberg: GIM-Verlag.

Füller, J., & Hutter, K. (2012). „Im Spiel liegt die Wahrheit" – Games zur Insights-Generierung. *Marketing Review St. Gallen, 29*(2), 26–32.

Fullerton, T. (2008). *Game design workshop: A playcentric approach to creating innovative games*. Amsterdam, Boston: Elsevier Morgan Kaufmann.

Halan, S., Rossen, B., Cendan, J., & Lok, B. (2010). High score!—Motivation strategies for user participation in virtual human development. In J. Allbeck, N. Badler, T. Bickmore, C. Pelachaud & A. Safonova (Eds.), *Intelligent virtual agents* (pp. 482–488). Berlin, Heidelberg: Springer.

Heinemann, G. (2012). *Der neue Online-Handel: Erfolgsfaktoren und Best Practices*. Wiesbaden: Gabler.

Heinemann, G. (2013). *No-Line-Handel höchste Evolutionsstufe im Multi-Channeling*. Wiesbaden: Springer Gabler.

Janke, K. (2012). Die neue Lust am Mitmachen. In *mafo 2012* (pp. 8–10).

MacElroy, W., & Gray, M. (2003). IMRO online survey satisfaction research: A pilot study of salience-based respondent experience modeling. *Journal of Online Research*, 1–17.

Munzinger, U., & Wenhart, C. (2012). Markenerleben messen, managen, maximieren. In U. Munzinger & C. Wenhart (Eds.), *Marken erleben im digitalen Zeitalter* (pp. 147–167). Wiesbaden: Springer Fachmedien.

Plennert, S., & Robra-Bissantz, S. (2014). Ein Serious Game als neue qualitative Erhebungsmethode für die Customer Journey beim Automobilkauf. In *Informatik 2014 - Big Data - Komplexität meistern* (pp. 383–398).

Salen, K., & Zimmerman, E. (2004). *Rules of play: Game design fundamentals*. Cambridge, Mass: MIT Press.

Sawyer, B., & Smith, P. (2008). Serious games taxonomy. In *Game Developers Conference*. http://www.dmill.com/presentations/serious-games-taxonomy-2008.pdf. Accessed August 29, 2014.

Schell, J. (2008). *The art of game design: A book of lenses*. Amsterdam, Boston: Elsevier Morgan Kaufmann.

Singer, E., Groves, R. M., & Corning, A. D. (1999). Differential incentives: Beliefs about practices, perceptions of equity and effects on survey participation. *The Public Opinion Quarterly, 63*(2), 251–260.

TNS Infratest. (2010). Digital life 2010. http://2010.tnsdigitallife.com. Accessed December 18, 2014.

van Douwe, U. (2011). Kundenzufriedenheit fortwährend oder retrospektiv analysieren (Teil 2). *Research & Results, 5*, 30–32.

van Someren, M. W., Barnard, Y. F., & Sandberg, J. A. C. (1994). *The think aloud method: A practical guide to modelling cognitive processes*. London: Academic Press.

Wellner, A. S. (2003). The new science of focus groups. *American Demographics, 25*(2), 29–33.

Werbach, K., & Hunter, D. (2012). *For the win: How game thinking can revolutionize your business*. Philadelphia: Wharton Digital Press.

Witt, M., & Robra-Bissantz, S. (2012). Sparking motivation and creativity with "Online Ideation Games". In *GI-Jahrestagung* (pp. 1006–1023).

Witt, M., Scheiner, C., & Robra-Bissantz, S. (2011). Gamification of online idea competitions: Insights from an explorative case. In H.-U. Heiss (Ed.), *Informatik 2011*. Ges. für Informatik: Bonn.

Chapter 9
Engaging the Crowd of Stakeholders in Requirements Engineering via Gamification

Fabiano Dalpiaz, Remco Snijders, Sjaak Brinkkemper,
Mahmood Hosseini, Alimohammad Shahri and Raian Ali

Abstract *Requirements engineering* (RE) is a discipline that focuses on obtaining a specification for a system that fulfils the expectations of the stakeholders. Unfortunately, the current state of the practice reveals that only a few stakeholders are involved—mostly key clients and lead designers—while active stakeholders are not highly engaged. This lowers the chances of obtaining a system that fully fulfils the stakeholders' wishes. Gamification is an opportunity to increase the engagement of stakeholders in RE by establishing feedback loops that reward the useful participants, i.e., those who provide valuable contributions (requirements) for the system being designed. The related trend of crowdsourcing can be employed to maximise the number of participating stakeholders, by making RE a participatory activity where current and prospective users, developers, clients and analysts are involved. This chapter introduces the *Crowd-Centric Requirements Engineering* (CCRE) method that guides software producing organisations (SPOs) by involving a crowd of engaged stakeholders in RE. CCRE uses the *REfine* tool, a gamified platform for eliciting and refining requirements. In addition to presenting the method and its application in a case study, we define research challenges for the field.

9.1 Introduction

The involvement of stakeholders in design and engineering endeavours is renowned. In management science, it was shown early on that user participation can overcome resistance to change (Zand and Sorensen 1975). In *requirements*

F. Dalpiaz (✉) · R. Snijders · S. Brinkkemper
Department of Information and Computing Sciences, Utrecht University, Utrecht
The Netherlands
e-mail: f.dalpiaz@uu.nl

M. Hosseini · A. Shahri · R. Ali
Faculty of Science and Technology, Bournemouth University, Poole, UK

© Springer International Publishing Switzerland 2017
S. Stieglitz et al. (eds.), *Gamification*, Progress in IS,
DOI 10.1007/978-3-319-45557-0_9

engineering (RE), the process that leads to the specification of a software system—user involvement—can improve system acceptance (Kujala 2003), diminish project failure (Emam et al. 1996; Kujala et al. 2005), deliver greater system understanding by the user (Damodaran 1996), and improve customer loyalty and broaden the market (Kabbedijk et al. 2009). Recent surveys identified user involvement as the most important success and failure factor for information technology projects (The Standish Group 2009).

The problem of stakeholder engagement is particularly hard for software producing organisations (SPOs), which guide the creation and evolution of software solutions that are delivered to multiple clients, as opposed to ad hoc software solutions that are tailored for one specific customer. The increased difficulty is due to the volume and diversity of requirements from the many clients, the challenge of aligning these requirements with the SPO's vision of and road map for the product, as well as the business concern of focusing on the key clients that generate most of the revenues (Lucassen et al. 2015a).

We propose relying on two pillars to maximise the engagement and participation of stakeholders in RE for software products: (i) *gamification* (Deterding et al. 2011) as a means to improve motivation, and, ultimately, quality (Eickhoff et al. 2012); and (ii) *crowdsourcing* to achieve higher, broader involvement through the outsourcing of a function to an undefined network of people by means of an open call (Howe 2006).

We go beyond existing works in the intersection of crowdsourcing and RE. The StakeRare method (Lim and Finkelstein 2012) uses the StakeSource 2.0 tool (Lim et al. 2011) to involve the crowd in requirements identification and prioritisation. A similar approach is the CrowdREquire platform (Adepetu et al. 2012). However, these platforms do not provide explicit means to motivate participants. On the other hand, the game-based collaborative tool iThink (Fernandes et al. 2012) helps collect new requirements and gain feedback on existing requirements; we take a step further by proposing an RE method where this type of tooling can be employed.

In this chapter, we present our method for crowd-centric, gamified RE that reconciles the desire of large user involvement with the business concerns of an SPO to satisfy key clients and to guide the evolution of its software products. The Crowd-Centric Requirements Engineering (CCRE) method that we describe realises our vision of a more participatory RE (Snijders et al. 2014) by employing the *REfine* gamified online platform for requirements elicitation and refinement (Snijders et al. 2015).

The rest of the chapter is structured as follows. In Sect. 9.2, we describe the method that we followed to construct the CCRE method. Section 9.3 describes the method as well as the *REfine* tool that supports it. In Sect. 9.4 we present research directions for the field, based on empirical studies that we conducted. Section 9.5 presents the conclusions.

9.2 Method Design

We followed a design science research approach (Peffers et al. 2007) for building and evaluating our proposed CCRE method and its support tool *REfine*. The literature played an essential role, as it was used not only to create the foundation of our method, but also to develop questions for a panel of experts who provided us with in-depth insights for devising CCRE. All details of the design process can be found in Snijders et al. (2015).

Ten experts participated in individual semi-structured interviews. Six experts worked in the software industry as advisors, technical directors or product managers, while four were researchers. The questions concerned three key topics: describing the current RE process, identifying room for improvement in RE, and defining success and failure factors for implementing crowdsourcing and gamification.

Each interview was recorded and summarised, after which the recommendations of the experts were extracted by tagging the key statements that the interviewees made. While some recommendations were literally stated, others were interpreted and rephrased by the researchers. This extraction led to 112 recommendations. Interviewees focused on varying areas, which were reflected in their recommendations. For example, one interviewee focused mainly on offline representation of users, whereas another interviewee was mainly interested in crowdsourcing and gamification aspects.

After an initial mapping of the recommendations on categories that resulted from our literature study, several categories contained many recommendations (e.g., user involvement and gamification elements) and a number of recommendations overlapped (e.g., 'Involve users to understand what the real problems are' and 'Involve real users not representatives'). These results were then organised into a revised set of categories and recommendations, while keeping track of the number of times a recommendation was given. The 68 resulting recommendations were the direct input for our method development.

9.3 The CCRE Method

Based on the expert recommendations, we carried out a rigorous method engineering process (Brinkkemper 1996) to augment traditional methods for RE with elements that enable realising the vision of crowd-centric RE. The resulting CCRE method includes seven phases, as shown in Fig. 9.1. A complete explanation of all activities within the phases can be found online (Snijders et al. 2015).

9.3.1 Feasibility Analysis

The goal of this phase is to determine the applicability of CCRE for the specific situation. It is therefore positioned as the very first step of CCRE to prevent

Fig. 9.1 The CCRE method.
Iterations also exist between
and within the phases. The
bottommost phase shows the
connection to development,
but is not part of CCRE itself

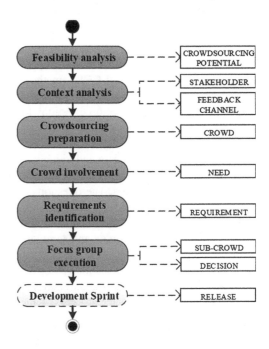

allocating resources to low-potential endeavours. Applicability is determined in terms of the potential of crowdsourcing and gamification for the product at hand.

Firstly, the scope of the method is defined: what is the area that CCRE will be applied to? While in one situation it might be useful for the long-term product roadmapping, in another context CCRE may be applied only to the product user interface. Three other aspects are then determined: (i) the SPO's future vision for that specific scope, (ii) the degree of openness of the SPO to the crowd's inputs, and (iii) situational factors that impact the effectiveness of crowdsourcing and gamification. The potential for crowdsourcing is concluded and results are made using a go/no-go decision.

CCRE would be unsuitable for a product with very few clients and for which the SPO has a clear vision and low openness to the crowd. On the other hand, CCRE would suit a product with numerous customers, low vision, and high openness.

9.3.2 Context Analysis

This phase analyses the context of the requirements elicitation, by identifying candidate stakeholders to involve in crowdsourcing (users, developers, analysts, clients, regulatory bodies, etc.) as well as the existing channels they can currently use to provide feedback.

A primary interactive platform is selected and a community manager is appointed to moderate the inputs and oversee the process. Our *REfine* tool is a possible platform that was designed for CCRE. Secondary channels have to be monitored too (e.g., e-mail, forums, etc.), as some users are likely to bypass the primary channel.

9.3.3 Crowdsourcing Preparation

Before initiating the actual crowd involvement, the crowd has to be formed, its characteristics assessed and its members prepared for the process. To mobilise stakeholders, the existence of the interactive platform has to be communicated and an incentive to be part of the community has to be provided through a marketing campaign.

The CCRE method should provide adequate incentives through the choice and implementation of gamification elements. The adequacy of the elements is domain specific (Nicholson 2012). The experts we interviewed suggested exploration, group formation, roles and rewards as useful techniques. The literature study has identified important elements such as *accelerated feedback cycles, clear goals and rules of play, a compelling narrative, challenging tasks* (Gartner 2011), *situated motivational affordance, universal design for learning,* and *player-generated content* (Nicholson 2012). Pointification in the form of points, leaderboards and achievements can provide a short-term incentive (Hamari et al. 2014).

Our gamified platform *REfine* is illustrated in Fig. 9.2. Apart from the home-, about-, leaderboards- and contact pages, *REfine* contains three important pages: the *needs overview, need details,* and *user profile*. On the menu bar, besides the hyperlinks to other pages, the user status bar shows the coins and points of the user.

Six types of gamification elements are implemented, each positively contributing to one or more social factors (Hamari and Koivisto 2013):

- *Roles* contribute to network exposure and reciprocal benefit: *ideator* of new needs, *commenter* on existing needs, and *assessor* by voting (like/dislike) on needs. The proficiency in a role is represented by points.
- *Resources and points* contribute to recognition and reciprocal benefit. Points are directly earned by adding needs, commenting, and voting, and indirectly when other participants vote or comment on created needs. Resources are expressed via coins that are required to perform actions.
- *Leaderboards* contribute to recognition. There are three types of leaderboards: (i) for each of the roles, (ii) for individual needs, and (iii) global.
- *Group formation* contributes to network exposure and social influence. Group formation is stimulated by the transparency of the stakeholder's background, and the separation of leaderboards per need.

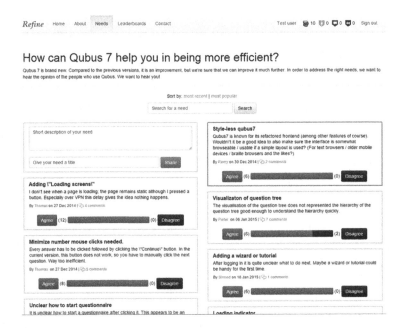

Fig. 9.2 The needs overview of *REfine*

- *Exploration* supports network exposure. Although minimally implemented in *REfine*: stakeholders can expand needs suggested by others and explore those traces.
- *Endorsements* favour social influence, recognition, and reciprocal benefit. Votes and comments have the function of endorsements that support/detract from a proposed need and provide more details/opinions, respectively.

9.3.4 Crowd Involvement

This is the phase where crowdsourcing and gamification occur. The crowd of stakeholders share their needs with each other through the use of the interactive platform. Since the aim is to let stakeholders learn from others and reach consensus, the crowd can discuss the suggested needs, using comments and need branching/merging. This latter functionality (supported by *REfine*) prevents users from hijacking existing needs and instead motivates them to improve them. This discussion activity enables explicit requirements negotiation, a largely overlooked phase in traditional RE. The crowd should also be able to communicate if they agree or disagree with the suggested needs. In line with the work of Berander and Andrews (2005), CCRE proposes that the simplest appropriate technique should be chosen for prioritisation.

During crowd involvement, the crowd should be engaged and tuned by the community manager to ensure that the incentives fit the crowd's characteristics. Stakeholders will probably bypass the chosen channel; as such, feedback mining techniques should be adopted to gather valuable needs. Social media analysis techniques such as opinion mining (Dave et al. 2003) and sentiment analysis (Pang and Lee 2008) could be employed to process such semi-structured feedback.

9.3.5 Requirements Identification

The needs that were suggested, discussed, and voted upon are candidate requirements for the product. Product managers and requirements engineers of the software product are involved, due to their knowledge about technical and business feasibility.

While sometimes mapping a need for a requirement may be easy, in other cases the need may still be vague (e.g., 'I want to have a more usable interface'). In the latter case, the involvement of the product management is key to understanding the need, refining it, and generating concrete solutions, working towards a product requirement.

In *requirements identification*, we distinguish between mainstream requirements, which are supported by a significant part of the crowd, and minority requirements, which have a smaller backing but are important for certain subgroups of the crowd. *Requirements priority* (Wiegers 1999) is based on their business value if implemented, the penalty if excluded, the implementation costs, and the risk for the business.

9.3.6 Focus Group Execution

Focus groups are organised for the requirements with higher business priority and stakeholder value. The focus groups further develop the requirements by exploring alternative design options. The most active stakeholders for those requirements are invited, including the ideator and most active contributors, while the SPO develops design options for the requirements and evaluates their quality, ruling out the low-quality ones.

9.4 Research Challenges

We present research directions that originate from a case study with CCRE in Sect. 9.4.1 and from empirical studies with domain experts in Sect. 9.4.2 of this chapter.

9.4.1   Challenges from a Case Study with CCRE

We have applied CCRE to a beta version of the Qubus 7 Governance Risk and Compliance (GRC) tool (http://www.qubussoftware.com/), a web platform for compliance auditors to conduct their assessment activities with customers. The study involved 19 participants (product managers, developers, experts, clients, end-users, prospective clients) who expressed 21 needs, 37 comments and 130 votes through *REfine* over the course of one month. Three mainstream needs and one minority need were analysed by the SPO, and three of them were further discussed in focus groups with the top contributors according to the need-specific leaderboards. More details are available in Snijders et al. (2015).

The users of *REfine* found the process to be less difficult, more useful and more engaging compared with previous feedback experiences. They felt motivated and thought that their input would be taken into account, but they thought that their priorities were not clearly presented to the SPO. They stated that the most common activities they performed were reading the needs and providing suggestions. The participants took little notice of the points and leaderboards on the platform, but largely agreed with the statement that the game elements made the experience more pleasant. Voting and commenting were considered very useful, while the utility of branching needs was rated neutrally.

In line with the findings by Hosseini et al. (2015), the experiment showed the difficulty of engaging a large number of participants, especially clients and end-users of the software product. An interview with two members of the Qubus product management revealed further challenges for our method and tool, including little incentive to return to the platform and the risk that novice participants would suggest trivial needs.

We also consulted with three external software product managers with experience in RE that responded to statements after a presentation of the method, prototype and the requirements obtained from the case study. They identified further challenges, observing that the quality of requirements would not be significantly better than the quality of the experts' methods, and the requirements may not be detailed enough for a focus group or Product Backlog. This risk could be mitigated through the use of tools that increase the quality of requirements expressed via simple formalisms such as user stories (Lucassen et al. 2015b). The risk of a non-representative crowd was also mentioned, as well as the different vocabulary of developers and end-users.

9.4.2   Challenges from Empirical Studies

The use of crowdsourcing and gamification poses several general challenges, such as the quality of the obtained results from the crowd and the compatibility of gamification design with user types and work environment. Besides the well-known challenges, the application of gamified crowdsourcing for RE introduces nuances and peculiarities mainly about the quality of requirements elicited and their trust-worthiness. The challenges presented in this section have been extracted from two different empirical studies, the first one involving 14 users and 34 experts in RE (Hosseini et al. 2015) and the second involving 12 employees and managers, and 30 experts in gamification (Shahri et al. 2014).

Challenges of applying crowdsourcing for RE

Crowdsourcing typically introduces a diverse crowd into RE, and such diversity may render decision-making processes harder to achieve, as several conflicting requirements may be stated by the crowd. Furthermore, such diversity makes it difficult to aggregate the results and developing an agreed upon approach satis-factory to all is naturally difficult. In addition, the lack of systematic approaches to aggregation also makes it difficult to trace an individual's requirements in the final aggregated requirements model.

Involving a crowd with different levels of competence is also necessary for the comprehensiveness of elicited requirements and their accommodation of both novice and more expert users. Without a proper balance among stakeholders with different competence levels, requirements engineers may only be able to elicit certain types of requirements, neglecting requirements from other types. Creating and measuring such a balance poses another challenge for requirements engineers.

Collaboration among stakeholders can also lead to dominance of certain opin-ions and clustering among the crowd providing the requirements. Dominance of crowd members happens when they have some authority, e.g., managers and their employees in the same forum, or when they use persuasive and influential language to deceive others (e.g., assertions). Clustering among stakeholders arises when each cluster tries to enforce their own viewpoints/needs on the requirements elicitation system.

Finally, keeping the crowd informed about their activities during RE processes via feedback channels can prove to be difficult as feedback should be timely, meaningful and comprehensible and should not interrupt stakeholders' activities or cause them information overload, which is, for some, as bad as the lack of information.

Challenges of applying gamification for RE

Gamification of RE processes has technical and organisational costs and expenses. Also, as gamification is not a 'one-size-fits-all' solution, it can adversely affect the process instead of supporting it. The engineering of gamification is challenging in the set of expertise it requires, necessitating the involvement of people from dif-ferent domains, such as behavioural economics, psychology and human-computer interaction. Such diverse expertise is key to ensuring properties such as compati-bility of game mechanics with the nature of requirements being elicited and the organisation's norms and culture.

Gamification is considered to be a performance-changing approach by adding motivation in a given work environment. An ad hoc design of gamification can have major effects on the users and lead to lower performance compared to a non-gamified process. This could mean, among other things, fewer elicited requirements, e.g., when stakeholders prefer to be commenters and not ideators in order to get points faster, and inappropriate requirements prioritisation, e.g., when top requirements in the list get more hits because they are more easily accessible.

Stakeholders should also be able to choose to not use gamification and this introduces new challenges as well, e.g., when gamification is rooted in the requirements elicitation system and is an integral part of it, and when a stakeholder or a user is an introvert who does not embrace some of the applied game mechanics. In the latter case, the introvert stakeholder may actually perform less efficiently, e.g., identify fewer requirements, in order not to appear in leaderboards and get social recognition.

Gamification can negatively influence the trustworthiness of elicited requirements as certain users may only participate for the sake of the rewards. Furthermore, gamification can also adversely affect stakeholders' intrinsic motivation in the RE process. This means that gamification may replace intrinsic motivations with some game elements, which usually have a shorter motivation life span, and when these game elements are removed from the requirements elicitation system, stakeholders may no longer feel motivated and engaged.

Finally, gamification should adapt to the characteristics and preferences of different stakeholders' characteristics, such as age, gender, culture and competitiveness of game mechanics, if a successful implementation of gamification is to be achieved. Different people are motivated in different ways and the gamification process should adapt accordingly to their personal characteristics and preferences.

9.5 Conclusion

In this chapter, we argued that the quality of the RE process, and of the resulting requirements, can be significantly improved by opening participation in RE to *all* stakeholders, including current and potential end-users, developers, clients, etc. In order to conduct this participatory RE process, we presented the CCRE method that employs *gamification* as a mechanism to engage stakeholders into an organised crowd and to keep them motivated throughout the RE process.

Our results showed that the discussions between the involved stakeholders produced requirements that were perceived as useful, and that *REfine* helped the refinement process leading to more accurate requirements. More evidence, however, should be collected by conducting experiments that isolate the treatment factor (gamification) from other factors such as the user interface.

To have a more holistic view in this study, we recognise the need to address further aspects of the method. The first one concerns the diversity in personality of the stakeholders. The personality traits discussed in the contribution from Costa and MacCrae (1992) should be considered while designing a gamified platform for requirements elicitation, as the success of the design highly relies on the perception of the stakeholders using it (Shahri et al. 2014). For example, while extrovert users may openly express their requirements in a forum where managers can see their feedback, introverts may refrain from doing so. As a result, the design of gamification should provide various features appropriate for motivating both introverts and extroverts. Another aspect concerns whether the gamified platform is being used to elicit requirements for a new software system or for evolution of an existing software system. For developing new software systems, the gamification design should consider game elements that stimulate more creativity in the users. For example, the choice of *time pressure* as a game element can hinder creativity because it may increase stress on those performing the gamified task. The last point concerns the involvement of a larger sample of stakeholders in the gamified platform. Utilising a large crowd allows for the discovery of several aspects related to crowd dynamics, such as collective behaviour and increased diversity (Hosseini et al. 2015). For example, a highly diverse set of stakeholders can lead to elicitation of more relevant, meaningful requirements and an increase in creativity, while it can also result in difficulties in reaching a consensus and may also yield more inconsistent requirements.

We have also sketched research directions that derive from a case study with CCRE and from other empirical studies. Future work should focus on those directions with particular attention to the development of group dynamics through the proactive support of tools such as *REfine*. We see gamification and crowdsourcing as a paradigm shift towards openness and engagement in RE, but their effectiveness requires reconsidering and tuning current RE methods for such a context.

Acknowledgments This research was partially supported by a European FP7 Marie Curie grant (the SOCIAD Project).

References

Adepetu, A., Ahmed, K. A., Al Abd, Y., Al Zaabi, A., & Svetinovic, D. (2012). CrowdREquire: A requirements engineering crowdsourcing platform. In *Proceedings of the AAAI Spring Symposium: Wisdom of the Crowd*.

Berander, P., & Andrews, A. (2005). Requirements prioritization. In *Engineering and managing software requirements* (pp. 69–94). Springer.

Brinkkemper, S. (1996). Method engineering: Engineering of information systems development methods and tools. *Information and Software Technology, 38*(4), 275–280.

Costa, P. T., & MacCrae, R. R. (1992). *Revised NEO personality inventory (NEO PI-R) and NEO five-factor inventory (NEO FFI): Professional manual*. Psychological Assessment Resources.

Damodaran, L. (1996). User involvement in the systems design process-a practical guide for users. *Behaviour & Information Technology, 15*(6), 363–377.

Dave, K., Lawrence, S., & Pennock, D. M. (2003). Mining the peanut gallery: Opinion extraction and semantic classification of product reviews. In *Proceedings of the 12th international conference on World Wide Web* (pp. 519–528). ACM.

Deterding, S., Dixon, D., Khaled, R., & Nacke, L. (2011). From game design elements to gamefulness: defining gamification. In *Proceedings of the 15th international academic MindTrek conference: Envisioning future media environments* (pp. 9–15). ACM.

Eickhoff, C., Harris, C. G., de Vries, A. P., & Srinivasan, P. (2012). Quality through flow and immersion: gamifying crowdsourced relevance assessments. In *Proceedings of the 35th international ACM SIGIR conference on Research and development in information retrieval* (pp. 871–880). ACM.

El Emam, K., Quintin, S., & Madhavji, N. H. (1996). User participation in the requirements engineering process: An empirical study. *Requirements Engineering, 1*(1), 4–26.

Fernandes, J., Duarte, D., Ribeiro, C., Farinha, C., Pereira, J. M., & da Silva, M. M. (2012). iThink: A game-based approach towards improving collaboration and participation in requirement elicitation. *Procedia Computer Science, 15*, 66–77.

Gartner. (2011). Gartner says by 2015, more than 50 percent of organizations that manage innovation processes will gamify those processes. http://www.gartner.com/newsroom/id/1629214. Last accessed February 19, 2016.

Hamari, J., & Koivisto, J. (2013). Social motivations to use gamification: An empirical study of gamifying exercise. In *Proceedings of the European Conference on Information Systems*.

Hamari, J., Koivisto, J., & Sarsa, H. (2014). Does gamification work?–A literature review of empirical studies on gamification. In *Proceedings of the 47th Hawaii International Conference on System Sciences (HICSS)* (pp. 3025–3034). IEEE.

Hosseini, M., Shahri, A., Phalp, K., Taylor, J., Ali, R., & Dalpiaz, F. (2015). Configuring crowdsourcing for requirements elicitation. In *Proceedings of the IEEE 9th International Conference on Research Challenges in Information Science (RCIS)* (pp. 133–138). IEEE.

Howe, J. (2006). Crowdsourcing: A definition (Online). http://www.crowdsourcing.com/cs/2006/06/crowdsourcinga.html. Last accessed February 19, 2016.

Kabbedijk, J., Brinkkemper, S., Jansen, S., & Van der Veldt, B. (2009). Customer involvement in requirements management: lessons from mass market software development. In *Proceedings of the 17th IEEE International Requirements Engineering Conference* (pp. 281–286). IEEE.

Kujala, S. (2003). User involvement: A review of the benefits and challenges. *Behaviour & information technology, 22*(1), 1–16.

Kujala, S., Kauppinen, M., Lehtola, L., & Kojo, T. (2005). The role of user involvement in requirements quality and project success. In *Proceedings of the 13th IEEE International Requirements Engineering Conference* (pp. 75–84). IEEE.

Lim, S. L., Damian, D., & Finkelstein, A. (2011). StakeSource2.0: Using social networks of stakeholders to identify and prioritise requirements. In *Proceedings of the 33rd International Conference on Software Engineering* (pp. 1022–1024). ACM.

Lim, S. L., & Finkelstein, A. (2012). Stakerare: Using social networks and collaborative filtering for large-scale requirements elicitation. *IEEE Transactions on Software Engineering, 38*(3), 707–735.

Lucassen, G., Dalpiaz, F., Van Der Werf, J. M., & Brinkkemper, S. (2015a). Bridging the twin peaks: the case of the software industry. In *Proceedings of the Fifth International Workshop on Twin Peaks of Requirements and Architecture* (pp. 24–28). IEEE.

Lucassen, G., Dalpiaz, F., van der Werf, J. M. E., & Brinkkemper, S. (2015b). Forging high-quality user stories: Towards a discipline for agile requirements. In *Proceedings of the 23rd IEEE International Requirements Engineering Conference* (pp. 126–135). IEEE.

Nicholson, S. (2012). A user-centered theoretical framework for meaningful gamification. In *Proceedings of Games+Learning+Society 8.0*.

Pang, B., & Lee, L. (2008). Opinion mining and sentiment analysis. *Foundations and Trends in Information Retrieval, 2*(1–2), 1–135.

Peffers, K., Tuunanen, T., Rothenberger, M. A., & Chatterjee, S. (2007). A design science research methodology for information systems research. *Journal of Management Information Systems, 24*(3), 45–77.

Shahri, A., Hosseini, M., Phalp, K., Taylor, J., & Ali, R. (2014). Towards a code of ethics for gamification at enterprise. In *Proceedings of the IFIP WG 8.1 Working Conference on the Practice of Enterprise Modeling* (pp. 235–245). Springer.

Snijders, R., Dalpiaz, F., Brinkkemper, S., Hosseini, M., Ali, R., & Oˇzum, A. (2015). REfine: A gamified platform for participatory requirements engineering. In *Proceedings of the 1st IEEE International Workshop on Crowd-Based Requirements Engineering* (pp. 1–6). IEEE.

Snijders, R., Dalpiaz, F., Hosseini, M., Shahri, A., & Ali, R. (2014). Crowd-centric requirements engineering. In *Proceedings of the Second Workshop on Crowdsourcing and Gamification in the Cloud (CGCloud)* (pp. 614–615). IEEE.

The Standish Group. (2009). CHAOS summary 2009: The 10 laws of CHAOS. Technical report.

Wiegers, K. (1999). First things first: Prioritizing requirements. *Software Development, 7*(9), 48–53.

Zand, D. E., & Sorensen, R. E. (1975). Theory of change and the effective use of management science. *Administrative Science Quarterly*, 532–545.

Part III
Gamification and Learning

Chapter 10
Reading with a Touch of Gameplay: Gamified E-Books' Convergence with Classical Literary Worlds

Răzvan Rughiniş and Cosima Rughiniş

Abstract Gamified e-books extend invitations for young and adult readers to revisit classical literary worlds. We examine ten e-books to discover distinctive rhetorical resources used to enhance the reading experience and achieve convergence with the original literary world. We distinguish between attempts to focus attention on the material world, to create empathy with characters through perception, choice and emotions and, last but not least, to shape the reader's journey through the medium of text. Our proposed inventory may guide designers in creating gamified e-books that bring literary worlds and characters to life even more vividly.

10.1 Introduction

Gamified or interactive e-books have been widely discussed in the context of the reading literacy challenge in the digital age. They have been proposed as a solution to encourage children to read by bridging the familiar visual and interactive media of videos, digital games and apps with the increasingly less familiar medium of text. In this line of reflection, researchers have investigated whether interactive e-books promote better literacy compared with the more traditional printed books: do they facilitate or hinder children's understanding of the narrative and the acquisition of new vocabulary? For example, a recent meta-analysis of the effects of technology-enhanced stories on young children literacy development (Takacs et al. 2015) concluded that there is a small but significant positive effect, in the aggregate, of multimedia features of e-books, specifically animated illustrations, music and sound effects. On the contrary, authors found that interactive elements, such as

R. Rughiniş (✉)
University Politehnica of Bucharest, Bucharest, Romania
e-mail: razvan.rughinis@cs.pub.ro

C. Rughiniş
University of Bucharest, Bucharest, Romania
e-mail: cosima.rughinis@sas.unibuc.ro

© Springer International Publishing Switzerland 2017
S. Stieglitz et al. (eds.), *Gamification*, Progress in IS,
DOI 10.1007/978-3-319-45557-0_10

139

hotspots or minigames, do not add, in the aggregate, to story comprehension and expressive vocabulary. Furthermore, they erased the positive effects of multimedia elements, suggesting that they can distract children from following the story.

We start our inquiry from an alternate departure point and readership—namely, the challenge of (re)acquainting oneself with classical literary worlds. We are interested in how interactive e-books may contribute to young and adult readers' interaction with well-known literary works such as Cervantes' *Don Quixote*, Shakespeare's *Hamlet*, Carroll's *Alice in Wonderland*, Poe's *horror stories*, Shelley's *Frankenstein*, Verne's journeys or Doyle's *Sherlock Holmes* investigations.

Why focus on classical works? To use Burke's analogy, literature offers us equipment for living (Burke 1998)—delineating the symbolic infrastructure which supports our self-constructs and our understanding of others in social situations. Classical literature also fulfils an additional function, becoming a resource for conversation with others. References to classical universes can be found in many instances—from school, where they occupy a privileged place, to the day-to-day cultural ambient of entertainment, documentation and other forms of reflection. *Classical literary worlds* offer people clues for understanding and pretexts for discussing one's own and others' passions and worldviews, real and imagined histories and geographies and, not in the least, aesthetic experiences.

10.2 Gamified E-Books' Convergence with Literary Worlds

Exploring *classical literary worlds* can be a lifelong pursuit, as it is by no means limited to childhood or school years. At the same time, adults as well as children are offered a huge variety of cultural products (e.g., books); the competition for our time remains intense throughout the years. We may find ourselves not as willing to make time to read or re-read *The Tragedy of Hamlet, Prince of Denmark*, or *Alice's Adventures in Wonderland*. Interactive e-books offer us an invitation to re-engage with these works—an invitation that extends to younger and older adults alike. They give a pretext to revisit famous characters' worlds and stories. We therefore aim to answer the following question: What are the specific affordances of interactive e-books for exploring (classical) literary worlds?

The term *interactive e-books* is often used interchangeably with other descriptions, such as '*technologically enhanced books*' (Takacs et al. 2015) or '*e-storybooks*' (Moody 2010). E-books that require the reader to co-author the text by choosing between different storylines are also referred to as '*gamebooks*'. In this chapter we focus on gamified e-books, which include both text and gameful or playful interactive elements, beyond the e-book interface needed for advancing through the text (such as scrolling or page turning). Such interactive elements may consist of interactive illustrations or calligraphy, in choosing how the story unfolds, or in minigames inserted throughout the story, such as puzzles or hidden object games.

We start from a definition of gamification for learning contexts as *simple gameplay to support productive interaction for expected types of learners and instructors* (Rughiniş 2013b). Our core concept is *simple gameplay*—that is, we look into e-books that offer a certain interactivity that can be experienced as gameplay. We thus include, under this concept, both e-books that afford gameful orientations, in the stricter, design-focused definition proposed by Deterding et al. (2011), and those that afford playful orientations less bound by rules and goals, covered by the broader term *playification* (Scott 2014).

Gamification has often been examined in light of motivational design and re-alignment of interests (Rughiniş 2013b). While some researchers are very critical of gamification's rhetoric, assumptions and uses (Bogost 2011, 2014), others accept the term and examine the variability of its situated use (Deterding 2011; Llagostera 2012; Rughiniş 2013a), aiming to disentangle the ethical and unethical, as well as the desired and undesired consequences of gamified activities.

The dark side of gamification can be clearly distinguished in marketing contexts, when customers may be incentivised to spend money or disclose personal information against their better judgement. The stakes seem different when we look into the gamification of books, as there is less potential for exploiting readers. Still, gamification runs the risks of actually degrading, rather than enhancing, the experience by distracting attention from the story and from reading (Korat and Shamir 2004; Martens 2015; Takacs et al. 2015). Two important dimensions on which gamified books can be evaluated refer, thus, to their convergence with the story, on the one hand, and their use of the medium of text, on the other hand.

Convergence, or the capacity to enhance rather than distract from the narrative (Martens 2015), is considered a key element for assessing an interactive e-book (Korat and Shamir 2004; Takacs et al. 2015). We aim to contribute to the designers' and users' capacity to evaluate convergence, which we conceptualise in two dimensions:

- Convergence through enactments of material worlds;
- Convergence through enactments of subjective worlds.

For example, when examining the possibilities of translating *Sherlock Holmes* into a game, Fernandez-Vara (2013) proposed a list of *core behaviours that define the character*, such as Holmes using sources efficiently, employing science and vast knowledge, displaying a keen perception and a mastery of chemistry, using deception and disguises, smoking and using drugs, and fighting (pp. 4–5). These behaviours could be modelled by inserting the defining material inventory (sources of information, chemical substances, disguised clothing, pipes and guns, among others) into the game and then putting the player in the position to see and act upon the world through them.

When examining material worlds, we look at how gamified books invite readers to re-create the material universe of the literary work, including a general material ambient, on the one hand, and specific objects that play a key role in the story, on the other hand—for example Fogg's suitcases, the artificial body created in *Frankenstein*, the *drink-me* bottle in *Alice*, or the *oval portrait* in Poe's tale with the same title.

Regarding subjective worlds, we investigate the gamified e-books' ability to foster readers' empathy with literary characters. Belman and Flanagan (2010) considered that games may encourage empathy with game characters on two dimensions: *cognitive* and *affective*. Taking this distinction into account to examine gamified e-books' affordances, we look into how they can offer resources for empathy by:

- Highlighting the characters' subjective perception of the world—that is, seeing the world *through their eyes*;
- Acting in the world by experiencing the characters' choices;
- Last but not least, feeling the characters' emotions—that is, 'walking in their shoes'.

We also examine the relevance of the medium of text. Bidarra et al. (2014, p. 283) mentioned the definitional issue on whether a gamified e-book is still a book, and they argued that in this genre 'non-textual elements should enhance, not replace text: they should not be the only source of engagement, they should rather foster readers' engagement with the text'. We take up this concern since we consider text a crucial element of classical literary worlds. Thus, we consider that it is important to be able to discuss and evaluate the possible uses of text in interactive e-books, and to enable users to choose products taking into account their relationships with text.

10.3   Method

In order to examine the specificities of the convergence between gamified e-books and classical literary worlds, we chose to study the interactive e-books available on Google Play that are related to well-known works. In Table 10.1, we present the list of these e-books, their relationship with the classical work they refer to, and their rhetorical resources on three dimensions: visual resources, aural resources and game mechanics.

We do not aim to evaluate each and every e-book regarding convergence; rather, we examine them in order to explore and discover remarkable, distinctive rhetorical resources to achieve convergence – as well as risks and limitations in doing so. In Table 10.2 we systematise our inventory, highlighting its distinctive resources and risks in focusing the reader's attention on the literary world it refers to, for each e-book.

Table 10.1 E-Books that refer to classical literary works on Android

E-book	Text	Visual resources		Aural resources		Game mechanics		
		Illustrations	Animated or interactive text	Read aloud	Soundtrack	Choice of narrative	Minigames	Reward for completion
The Adventures of Don Quixote (Touch of Classic 2013b)	Abridged	Animated Interactive	No	Yes	Page turning Object sounds Interactive music	No	Yes	Yes
To Be or Not to Be (North 2015)	Rewritten	Few Static	Text materiality	No	Music Screen taps	Yes	No	No
The Alice App (Paletz 2014)	Original	Animated Interactive	No	Yes	Object sounds	No	No	No
Frankenstein (Profile Books & inkle 2013)	Rewritten	Static	Text materiality	No	Page turning	Yes	No	No
Frankenstein (Touch of Classic 2013a)	Abridged	Animated	Text materiality	Yes	Page turning Music	No	No	Yes
iPoe Collection vol. 1 (iClassics Collection 2012)	Original	Animated Some interactivity	Variable calligraphy	No	Page turning, music, object sounds	No	No	No
80 Days (Profile Books & inkle 2014)	Rewritten	Animated Interactive	Moving text	No	Music, ambient noise	Yes	No	No
Around the World in 80 Days (Anuman 2015)	Abridged	Interactive (minigames)	No	No	Music Feedback	No	Yes	No
Journey to the Center of the Earth (L'Apprimerie 2014)	Original	Animated Interactive	Animated and interactive calligraphy	No	Music	No	No	No
Game is Afoot (Mobile Deluxe 2013)	Abridged	Interactive (minigames)	No	No	Music Feedback	No	Yes	No

Table 10.2 An inventory of resources for convergence between selected e-books and their literary worlds regarding the material universe, empathy, and text

Literary world	E-Book	Material universe	Resources for empathy with characters (vs. discordance)			The medium of text	
			Perception	Choice	Emotions	Calligraphy	Reading intensity
Cervantes' Don Quixote	ToC	Highlighting objects through animation and interactivity	Shifting perceptions: delusions Beauty through love				Low: line level, little text
Shakespeare's Hamlet	To Be or Not to Be			Choice of actions, but reframed and formulated humorously		Materiality of text	High: paragraph level, long text
Carroll's Alice in Wonderland	The Alice App	Highlighting objects, sizes and transformations through animation, interactivity and sound	Representing transformations of size and form				High: page level, long text
Poe's short horror stories	iPoe	Highlighting objects through animation, interactivity and sound	Representing core features of characters' perceived world: – sounds: heartbeat, clock ticking – mysterious light: oval portrait		Using animation, interactivity, music sounds and vibrations to achieve surprise and fear	Calligraphy: – shaping the flow of reading – representing or highlighting mental states: concentration, surprise	High: page level, medium text
Shelley's Frankenstein	ToC	Highlighting objects through animation and interactivity				Digital materiality of paragraphs	Medium: paragraph level, medium text

(continued)

Table 10.2 (continued)

Literary world	E-Book	Material universe	Resources for empathy with characters (vs. discordance)			The medium of text	Reading intensity
			Perception	Choice	Emotions	Calligraphy	
	Profile Books & Inkle		(Discordant aesthetic experience)			Materiality of text	High: paragraph and page level, long text
Verne's Around the world in 80 Days	Inkle	Exploring the material universe and objects' properties: size, commercial value, aggregation	Perceiving the globe through its affordances for travel, in a fictive world Salience of object size	Calculation and planning Managing human relationships	Emotions associated with – time pressure – success and failure	Animated calligraphy draws attention at how text is abridged and connected	Medium: paragraph level, long text
	Anuman	Rich material world risking overcrowding Highlighting objects through interactivity	(Discordant perception)		(Discordant emotions)		Low: line level, short text
Verne's Journey	Journey to the Center of the World	Highlighting objects through calligraphy, animation and interactivity	Experiencing the underground universe			Calligraphy – interactive calligraphy	High: page level, long text
Doyle's Holmes	Game is Afoot	Rich material world risking overcrowding Highlighting objects through interactivity	Perceiving the world as a container of clues		Concentration in search		Low: line level, short text

10.4   The Material Universe

Any illustrated book creates a visual representation of the material ambient of the story and highlights some of its elements for its readers. Interactive e-books use the specific features of animation, interactivity and sound to focus even more of the readers' attention on selected objects, their properties and transformations.

For example, the Alice App highlights the following elements through movement, interactivity and sound: the white rabbit's clock, the *drink-me bottle*, the *pepper*, the transformation of the baby into a pig, the vanishing *Cheshire cat*, and Alice's changing sizes.

These affordances raise the following question: Are the highlighted objects and environments central to the story world? For example, ToC's *Frankenstein* highlights the monster's assembled body, a core object of the narrative, through a minigame in which the reader discovers body parts throughout the book. On the other hand, *Game is Afoot* runs the risk of diverting the readers' attention from the storyline through its rich material universe that lacks clear selection criteria. Given that this e-book relies on hidden object minigames and puzzles, there is ample opportunity for discovering and interacting with different elements. Still, this also means that illustrations are very crowded with objects that bear little relevance to the story, other than belonging to the same period of time. Also, even when there is the possibility of convergence between the players' search activity and the story line, this opportunity may be ignored. For example, when, at one point in the game, the narrative asks *Do you know where the photograph is?*, the player is not actually required to find the photograph, but rather to discover five differences between two images, differences which are not relevant to this question.

The discordance between the story world and the e-book's material universe is stronger in Anuman's 80 *Days*, because the logic of finding hidden objects in landscapes crowded with stuff has little similarity to the situations faced by either Phileas Fogg or Passepartout in their journey. Some relevance could be created, for example, by requiring players to find and pack required items in the briefcase. On the other hand, this e-book also includes puzzles that require players to reconstitute a newspaper or a map, which are better linked to the storyline.

Profile Books & inkle's 80 *Days* recreates a relevant material world precisely through the items that the player, as Passepartout, buys in the market and packs in suitcases. These objects are described by their potential commercial value and size, thus enriching the readers' appreciation of the things that are part of this journey (see Figs. 10.1, 10.2 and 10.3).

Fig. 10.1 Three dimensions for examining convergence between gamified e-books and classical literary worlds

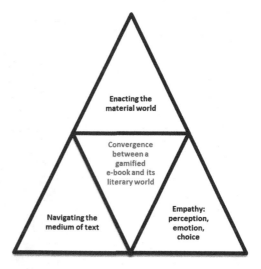

Fig. 10.2 Kindling surprise, fear, curiosity or jubilation through interactivity and game mechanics, in iPoe

Fig. 10.3 Animation and interactivity as resources for assembling material universes and highlighting objects with their properties and transformations. Shopping for items and packing in Profile Books & inkle's 80 Days

10.5 Empathy with Characters

By immersing readers into story worlds and opening up opportunities for them to perceive them as the characters do, to choose like them and to feel their emotions, gamified e-books offer opportunities to foster player empathy on cognitive, behavioural and emotional dimensions.

10.5.1 Empathy Through Perception

Animation and interactivity may illustrate, for readers, the characters' specific perceptual lenses. For example, the readers of ToC's *Don Quixote* notice how he sees himself in a mirror as a knight wearing glorious armour, but then, by wiping the mirror, they can also see an alternative, degraded appearance of the man, in his house garments that he wears underneath makeshift armour. Perceptive shifts are illustrated throughout the book through interactive pictures and switching musical backgrounds. Whether visual and musical switches encourage empathy with the hero, or limit it, it is an open question. Perceptual shifts may frame *Don Quixote*'s perceptions as delusional and unstable, undermining readers' empathy with the strong conviction and steadfastness in Quixote's worldview.

Animation and interactivity also shape other features of the characters' perceived world, such as the mystery created through changing light and colour (in iPoe), the salience of size (in Profile Books & inkle's 80 *Days*), or seeing the world as a container of clues (*Game is Afoot*). On the other hand, e-books may fail to convey the perceptive experience of a character: for example, Profile Books & inkle's *Frankenstein* includes an array of beautiful illustrations that do not capture the turning moment when Dr. Frankenstein suddenly ceases to see his creation as wonderful, and instead sees it as hideous (while ToC's *Frankenstein* illustrates this shift). The reader is left to recreate this moment of conversion using their imagination—which may not be detrimental after all.

10.5.2   Empathy Through Choice

Profile Books & inkle's 80 *Days* is a clear example of how a gamified e-book can offer readers gameplay choices that recreate the characters' choices: the reader as a player must ponder and select routes, transportation means, luggage items and financial actions for Passepartout and Fogg's journey around the world. These actions may, in turn, lead to success or failure.

Three of the selected e-books offer readers the possibility to choose between alternative story lines. Their strategies are quite divergent. 80 *Days* positions the player as Passepartout, who exercises choice in his narrated words and deeds. '*To Be or Not to Be*' offers the player first a choice of characters, and then a choice of actions—bearing in mind that the entire text, and thus the available actions, are rewritten in a parodic style, and that some choices will lead to narrative lines that diverge wildly from the original line. Profile Books & inkle's *Frankenstein* position the reader as an unseen companion and interlocutor of characters, offering a choice of actions to which the characters react. It remains an open question if, and to what extent, various approaches in designing the readers' choice of storyline foster empathy and other types of relationships with characters.

10.5.3   Empathy Through Emotions

Interactivity and game mechanics can be designed to stir emotions, which may in turn be congruent or divergent from the characters' emotions in the story. For example, iPoe seeks to surprise and frighten the reader, which is quite convergent with the characters' emotional experiences in Poe's *horror stories* (see Fig. 10.4). Profile Books & inkle's 80 *Days* invites the player to fret over time constraints, to

 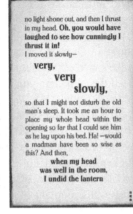 

(a) Profile Books & inkle's   (b) iPoe: variable calligraphy   (c) L'Apprimerie: interactive
Frankenstein   calligraphy

Fig. 10.4 Using digital materiality and animated calligraphy to shape the experience of reading texts. **a** Profile Books & inkle's *Frankenstein* **b** iPoe: variable calligraphy **c** L'Apprimerie: interactive calligraphy

rejoice for success or deplore failure—again, in alignment with Passepartout's emotions. Alternatively, the hidden-object account of Verne's *Around the World in 80 Days* is rather emotionally incongruent, since the gameplay dynamics for puzzle solving and finding hidden objects in heavily crowded landscapes diverges from situations in the story. Nonetheless, intense concentration for searching and jubilation when finding clues can be congruent with a detective's emotions, such as those in *Game is Afoot*.

10.6 Living in the Medium of Text

In order to describe the e-books' use of text, the first approach that comes to mind consists of measuring the ratio of reading to other actions, such as interacting with the e-book or gameplay. In Table 10.2 we sketch such a classification, distinguishing between e-books that include very short excerpts of text composed of several lines, e-books that present one or several paragraphs at a time, and e-books that include considerable, page-length amounts of texts. This classification combines two dimensions: (a) the total amount of text, and (b) the unit of text that is presented to the reader in between other actions. For example, *To Be or Not to Be* offers readers short fragments of text that are concatenated through readers' screen taps and choices, but the total amount of text is considerable. A similar strategy of fragmenting a long text into shorter units can be found in Profile Books & inkle's *Frankenstein*.

Another e-book strategy for drawing attention to text consists of creating a certain digital materiality for it. To illustrate, Profile Books & inkle's *Frankenstein* represents text as pieces of papers that are bound together by pins after the reader chooses the desired continuation (see Fig. 10.4a), while ToC's *Frankenstein* also includes text as floating, mobile pieces of paper.

Last but not least, e-books may use variable, animated or interactive calligraphy to shape the experience of reading, in the tradition of Apollinaire's calligrammes or Carroll's mouse-tail shaped poem. The iPoe stories (see Fig. 10.4b) and L'Apprimerie's Journey to the Center of the Earth (see Fig. 10.4c) best illustrate such creative and persuasive use of text.

10.7   Conclusion

Gamified e-books offer specific affordances for achieving convergence with the story worlds they refer to. By exploring ten interactive e-books related to classical literary works, we identified an inventory of rhetorical resources that can be used to enhance the medium of text, to highlight the material universe of the story and to highlight the characters' subjective experiences through perceptions, choices and emotions. Table 10.2 summarises the findings, highlighting both affordances and risks. A design approach that starts from a systematic classification of current convergence resources and issues may reach an even finer balance between text, multimedia and interactivity, and may also create novel ways to bring stories to life for a diverse group of readers.

References

Anuman. (2015). *Around the World in 80 Days*. https://play.google.com. Accesed July 1, 2015.
Belman, J., & Flanagan, M. (2010). Designing games to foster empathy. *Cognitive Technology, 14*(2), 5–15.
Bidarra, J., Natalio, C., & Figueiredo, M. (2014). Designing ebook interaction for mobile and contextual learning. In *2014 International Conference on Interactive Mobile Communication Technologies and Learning (IMCL2014)* (pp. 5–13). IEEE.
Bogost, I. (2011). *Persuasive games*. Exploitationware. Gamasutra.
Bogost, I. (2014). Why gamification is bullshit. In *The gameful world: Approaches, issues, applications* (pp. 65–78). MIT Press.
Burke, K. (1998). Literature as equipment for living. In D. H. Richter (Ed.), *The critical tradition. Classic texts and contemporary trends* (pp. 593–598). Boston: Bedford Books.
Deterding, S., et al. (2011). From game design elements to gamefulness: Defining "gamification". ACM (Ed.), *MindTrek'11* (pp. 9–15). Tampere, Finland: ACM Press.
Deterding, S. (2011). Situated motivational affordances of game elements: A conceptual model. In *CHI Conference on Human Factors in Computing Systems CHI 2011* (pp. 1–4). Vancouver: ACM.
Fernandez-Vara, C. (2013). The game's afoot: Designing Sherlock Holmes. In *Proceedings of DiGRA 2013* (pp. 1–14).

iClassics Collection. (2012). *iPoe Collection* (Vol. 1). https://play.google.com. Accesed July 1, 2015.

Korat, O., & Shamir, A. (2004). Do Hebrew electronic books differ from Dutch electronic books? A replication of a Dutch content analysis. *Journal of Computer Assisted learning, 20*(4), 257–268.

L'Apprimerie. (2014). *Journey to the Center of the Earth.* Illustrated by Julie Guilleminot. https://play.google.com. Accesed July 1, 2015.

Llagostera, E. (2012). On gamification and persuasion. In *Proceedings of SBGames 2012* (pp. 12–21).

Martens, M. (2015). Reading and "gamification": Joining guilds, earning badges, and leveling up. *Children and Libraries, 12*(4), 19.

Mobile Deluxe. (2013). *The game is afoot.* https://play.google.com. Accesed 1 July 2015.

Moody, A. K. (2010). Using electronic books in the classroom to enhance emergent literacy skills in young children. *Journal of Literacy & Technology, 11*(4), 22–52.

North, R. (2015). To be or not to be. Tin man games. https://play.google.com. Accesed July 1, 2015.

Paletz, E. (2014). *The Alice App.* https://play.google.com. Accesed July 1, 2015.

Profile Books & inkle. (2013). *Frankenstein.* https://play.google.com. Accesed July 1, 2015.

Profile Books & inkle. (2014). *80 Days.* https://play.google.com. Accesed July 1, 2015.

Rughiniş, R. (2013a). Flexible gamification in a social learning situation. In *10th International Conference on Computer Supported Collaborative Learning CSCL 2013* (pp. 137–140). Madison: ISLS.

Rughiniş, R. (2013b). Gamification for productive interaction. Reading and working with the gamification debate in education. In *The 8th Iberian Conference on Information Systems and Technologies CISTI 2013* (pp. 1–5). Lisbon: IEEE.

Scott, A. (2014). Meaningful Play: How Playcentric Research Methods are Contributing to New Understanding and Opportunities for Design. In P. A. Rogers & J. Yee (Eds.) *The Routledge companion to design research* (pp. 400–414). Routledge.

Takacs, Z. K., Swart, E. K., & Bus, A. G. (2015). Benefits and pitfalls of multimedia and interactive features in technology-enhanced storybooks: A meta-analysis. *Review of Educational Research*, 698–739.

Touch of Classic. (2013a). Frankenstein. https://play.google.com. Accesed July 1, 2015.

Touch of Classic. (2013b). The Adventures of Don Quixote. https://play.google.com. Accesed July 1, 2015.

Chapter 11
Gamification of Teaching in Higher Education

Dominik Siemon and Linda Eckardt

Abstract Gamification has become a major aspect in many fields of academia. Motivating people to participate and engage more intensively in order to increase the outcome with the help of game mechanics has already been applied in the field of education. With our approach of gamification of university teaching, we seek to improve the learning efficiency, motivation, fun and participation by constructing *GamEducation*. We implemented *GamEducation* in a master's level course, conducted it twice over two years and conducted several evaluations to validate our hypothesis. We found that *GamEducation* improves major fields of university teaching such as motivation, fun, participation and learning efficiency. However, *GamEducation* increases the workload for both students and teaching staff.

11.1 Introduction and Motivation

During recent years, gamification has gained considerable importance in many fields of academia. The integration of gamification in order to increase motivation, discipline and efficiency in education is not completely new (Lee and Hammer 2011). There are some examples of gamification in university teaching. *Creatures of the Night*, characterised as an environment of vampires and werewolves who have to fulfil missions to gain points for a lecture in Math (Kruse et al. 2014) and *The Legend of Zyren*, described as a group of students who form a guild for solving tasks, while collecting experience points for a lecture in Information Science (Knautz and Soubusta 2013), are such examples. However, these approaches focus on a background story, similar to a fairy-tale, in order to convey the learning material. These are not realistic problems which students will be confronted with in

D. Siemon (✉) · L. Eckardt
Institut für Wirtschaftsinformatik, Technische Universtität Braunschweig, Braunschweig, Germany
e-mail: d.siemon@tu-braunschweig.de

L. Eckardt
e-mail: linda.eckardt@tu-braunschweig.de

© Springer International Publishing Switzerland 2017
S. Stieglitz et al. (eds.), *Gamification*, Progress in IS,
DOI 10.1007/978-3-319-45557-0_11

their future professional lives. Although students are told to think critically when solving problems, there are not enough teaching concepts used at the university to reinforce this behaviour. Business games try to use critical thinking as a learning method. This can be defined as a combination of gaming and simulation, with features such as rules, competition and cooperation to give participants the possibility to act and gain experience within a fictitious but realistic environment (Greenblat and Duke 1981). For this reason, our objective is to integrate gamification into a more realistic background story in order to improve learning efficiency, motivation, fun and participation in university lectures.

11.2 Theoretical Foundations

In the following section, the theoretical basis of university teaching and gamification are explained.

11.2.1 University Teaching

Traditional university teaching methods, such as lecturing, means frontal teaching with few interactions, which is suitable for teaching information but does not stimulate interaction, additional thoughts or inspiration (Bligh 1998). Teaching is not the same as learning. Learning means using and applying knowledge and information (Bligh 1998; Laurillard 2002). Traditional university teaching provides the necessary information for the students to apply this information and learn independently. In seminars or smaller groups this information can be applied and transformed into learning results (Laurillard 2002).

Information and communication technology have revolutionised business and industry by giving people the opportunity to interact, communicate and collaborate. In contrast to this, university teaching and research have predominantly made use of communication tools, virtual learning environments, learning management systems and an improved computer infrastructure. The usage is still limited and attempts to blend information technology into all parts of university teaching (Selwyn 2007). Learning management systems (LMS) have rapidly emerged in the university teaching over the last few years (Coates et al. 2005). LMS implement administration functionalities, educational interaction and other pedagogical methods and should therefore complement the traditional university teaching. Despite their wide usage, LMS are criticised because of their restrictions, refusal of use, complexity, the reconstruction of established procedures and other effects on university teaching (Tolmie and Boyle 2000; Coates et al. 2005). Beyond communication and administration support, new approaches attempt to improve university teaching with the integration of game mechanics, actual game-based learning or business games. Different research results have shown that projects that integrate game mechanics achieve more motivation and enjoyment (Dickey 2007), but do not always result in increased learning efficiency (Jackson and McNamara 2013).

11.2.2 Game Mechanics and Gamification

The terms *game*, *game mechanics* and *gamification* should be explained in order to understand how they can be used for the redesign of lectures. The term *play* describes the creative activity of a person and involves problem solving behaviour, flexibility, learning and improvisation that lead to imagination (e.g., Dansky 1980; Russ 1996; Witt 2013). Games can be seen as a part of play, because often 'forms of play are looser and less organized than games' (Salen and Zimmerman 2004, p. 72). A game is characterised as an interactive system with a formal structure through defined rules that results in a measurable outcome for participation (e.g., Salen and Zimmerman 2004; Costikyan 2006; Sicart 2008). Gamification is currently a much-discussed method to use the potential of games and describes the integration of game design elements, such as game mechanics, into a non-game context (Deterding et al. 2011). Game mechanics are defined as actions of play allowed by the rules that can positively influence the players' behaviour and motivation to attain goals (e.g., Fullerton et al. 2004; Järvinen 2008). In our work, we focus on a few game mechanics according to Kim (2009) (see Fig. 11.1).

The system automatically awards participants game points for their specific behaviour (Hacker and Ahn 2009). Participants also obtain immediate feedback and benefit from the fact that all players get the same number of points for the same activity which leads to a form of competition and comparison (Witt 2013). In contrast to this, social points are not automatically given by the system but by other

Fig. 11.1 Game mechanics in this work (e.g., Kim 2009)

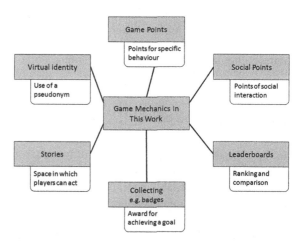

participants. Füller et al. (2010) distinguished an absolute from a relative judgement. A relative judgement allows players a pair-wise comparison (Füller et al. 2010). An absolute judgement means the players assign an absolute score. In this work an absolute judgement for awarding social points is used. The players' scores are represented in a ranking (Füller et al. 2010). The ranking position in the leaderboard allows the players to make comparisons with each other and is a form of feedback for them (Reeves and Read 2009). One way to support competition is to collect badges. Additionally, badges are often visualised graphically and symbolise an award for achieving a specific goal (Formanek 1991). Stories occur in a static or dynamic form. Background stories as used in this work are static and provide a space in which players can act (Mallon and Webb 2000). Conversely, dynamic stories are described as interactive types and players have the possibility to write their own story (Crawford 2004). The final game mechanic that we used for this work is virtual identity. In some cases, representation takes the form of an avatar and stands for a visual representation of the players' selves (Jin 2009). In our case, the virtual identity allows the player to be anonymous.

11.3 Application of Game Mechanics to University Teaching

Traditional university teaching mostly consists of frontal teaching where students experience difficulties concentrating during the lecture. Consequently, they do not understand the substantive context within a lecture and between a lecture series. On the one hand, playing can encourage learning and on the other hand it can improve a person's creativity while working (Webster and Martocchio 1992; Dickey 2007). Other motives for gamification are an increase in motivation and a strengthening of the social belongingness of participants (Witt 2013). Enhancing learner satisfaction through immediate feedback and individual achievable goals is another reason for gamification (McGonigal 2011). Therefore, it is our main goal to integrate game mechanics into university teaching in order to develop a more motivating environment that facilitates the students' learning.

11.3.1 GamEducation

We hypothesised that the gamification of university teaching increases motivation, participation and learning efficiency. In order to test this, we developed an individual and also applicable concept of gamification in education, *GamEducation*. The name *GamEducation* combines the words 'gamification' and 'education'. The central feature of *GamEducation* is not a game in the sense of a business or a simulation game, but the inclusion of game elements into the teaching process. The gameplay was set up such that it would create playful competition between students. The *GamEducation* concept was implemented in a specific master's level lecture with a certain number of students, but is also assignable to different teaching models, e.g., smaller seminars or workshops. The following section describes the concept and requirements in detail.

11.3.1.1 *GamEducation*—A Case Study

The *GamEducation* project was first implemented in the master's level lecture 'cooperation in e-business' in 2012. The lecture was a traditional two-hour frontal lecture with about 45 students. The lecture deals with strategic decisions and strategic planning in the electronics business, which involves all major partners of the company. Cooperation, coordination and communication processes between business partners are also discussed. The lecture explains the fundamentals of strategic design possibilities for all the important fields of e-business and illustrates them using practical examples.

For the purpose of *GamEducation* we shortened the reading material so as to be able to hold the lecture in four sessions. In addition to this we created a background story as a basis for the challenges. This background story introduces a fictional company which is looking for a new business segment that should be developed during the challenges. The challenges were created in close development with lecture material and were part of the group work. Six groups were formed at the beginning of the project made up of seven or eight members. Every lecture session was followed by one challenge. The topics of the lecture sessions and the challenge tasks were as follows: (a) e-business management and business model creation; (b) customer relationship management, supply chain management and network management; (c) communication, coordination and cooperation; (d) enterprise 2.0. Every challenge was presented one week after the equivalent lecture was held. We designed four additional ad hoc tasks, which created the opportunity to get individual points.

Along with the lecture sessions a blog system was made available to the students in order to give them the opportunity to gain additional points. Every student could post lecture related content and discuss different topics on this blog. The blog also integrated a current ranking for the groups and for each individual member. Alongside gaining points through the blog, the students could also earn points during the lecture sessions for comments and involvement in the discussion. The groups earned points for the presentation of their challenge. Points for the presentation were awarded by the teaching staff but also took the opinion of the remaining students into consideration. The students were asked to judge every challenge presentation except their own. Figure 11.2 shows the structure of the game:

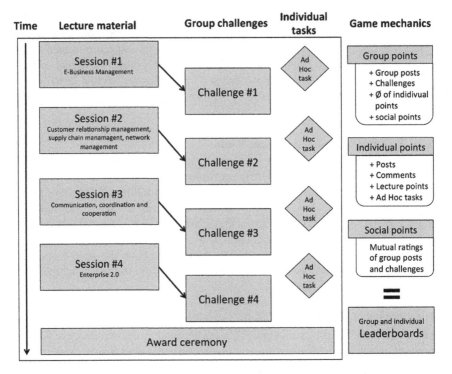

Fig. 11.2 *GamEducation* concept implemented in the 'cooperation in e-business' master lecture

In order to deploy one set of Kim's (2009) defined game mechanics we conducted an awards ceremony at the end of the project, honouring both the individuals and the group leaders. We handed out badges, i.e. medals (gold, silver and bronze), to the first three students from the leaderboard and to the top three groups.

During the first round of the project, the teaching staff experienced a large increase in mentoring and assistance work, for which an additional member of teaching staff was hired. In particular, the manual documentation of the game points greatly increased the workload. In addition, the previously used blog system did not satisfy the functionalities required by the *GamEducation* concept. Therefore, we developed a customised system able to automatically record all student interaction. This system was able to assign every student to a group and enable them to post articles and comments. Every contribution was automatically rated by the system and could be manually adjusted by the teaching staff at a later date. An automatically generated leaderboard for the individual ranking and group ranking shows the current points of every student. The system was used for the second time in 2013/2014 and significantly lightened the workload for the teaching staff. Before the second implementation we reduced the size of the teaching staff by one full time employee. In addition to this the use of the system increased the overall structure and transparency of the game.

11.3.1.2 Evaluation of GamEducation

Over the course of two years we conducted different evaluations concerning the experience, workload and student satisfaction. The *GamEducation* project was applied twice over two years and evaluations were carried out before, during and after the semester. In an initial survey, conducted before the lecture started, we asked 25 students about their prior experiences and their attitudes towards new approaches to university teaching. The majority of the students were open to trying new teaching approaches under the condition that the workload would not exceed the prior workload. Furthermore, we asked about the expected learning efficiency and increase of enjoyment during the lecture. 64 % expected a growth in learning efficiency and 92 % expected to have more fun as a result of the new teaching approach.

After the project was carried out for the first time we verified the prior expectations with 22 students and also conducted interviews with 10 students to obtain feedback. Our survey was divided into four main parts: (a) *learning efficiency*, (b) *workload*, (c) *motivation and fun* and (d) *participation and game mechanics*.

In part (a) we asked if (i) 'The new approach motivated me to participate more than usual'. 14 students agreed with this question, whereas six neither agreed nor disagreed (neutral) and just two students disagreed. In (ii) we asked if 'The application of the lecture material in the challenges helped me to better understand the overall content of the lecture'. In response to this question 15 students agreed, five neither agreed nor disagreed (neutral) and two students did not agree. Three more questions about the personal learning efficiency were asked in part (a), with which the students were mainly in agreement. Overall it can be summarised that the majority of the students experienced a highly increased learning efficiency thanks to *GamEducation*. Part (b) contained four questions concerning the workload of the lecture. The questions considered different elements of the approach, in particular the challenges, ad hoc tasks and the overall lecture. On average the answers were identical: the workload was (1) more than usual and (2) too high. However, six students agreed that the workload of the lecture in general was appropriate.

In part (c) we inquired about *satisfaction, motivation* and *enjoyment*. We asked (i) 'How satisfied were you with the overall new teaching approach?'. 15 students were satisfied, five were neutral and two students were not satisfied. Question (ii) stated 'I participated actively because I had fun gaining points'. 13 students agreed, six students neither agreed nor disagreed (neutral) and three students disagreed. Two questions were posed to find out whether they participated actively: (iii) 'Because I was interested in this field of study' and (iv) 'Because I wanted to get further insights in this field of study'. These questions prompted predominantly neutral answers, with a tendency towards agreement. Overall, the answers to part (c) were positive, with slightly more neutral responses concerning active participation. In spite of this, the majority of the students had fun and were satisfied with the lecture overall.

Part (d) evaluated the game mechanics in particular. Question (i) asked if 'I experienced the active participation as promoting the competition'. 15 students agreed with this question, three answered neutrally and only four disagreed. The majority of the students (7) neither agreed nor disagreed when asked question (ii): 'I participated actively, because I wanted to have a good position in the ranking'. Eight students agreed with this question and seven disagreed. However, more students agreed that they participated actively because they wanted their group to perform better in the rankings. In summary, the game mechanics led to more intense participation.

In addition to the survey we interviewed 10 students who had volunteered to participate. In general, they talked about the higher workload and agreed on the increase in participation due to the competition. Furthermore, they gave additional advice regarding the group size, the system we used during the first project and the rules and transparency of the ranking structure. Many students requested a better explanation and more transparency on how to gain points. Another important point of criticism was the system we used in the first round of the project. This led to the development of a customised individual system which supports the full structure and functionality of *GamEducation*. As previously mentioned, the system developed was used in the second round of the project.

After the second round with the newly developed system, we conducted another qualitative evaluation. In the second round we had a total of 51 students participating in the lecture and we conducted interviews with 20 students after the second round. Many aspects coincided with the first evaluation after the first round. In particular, the level of satisfaction, the experienced learning efficiency and the motivation were mainly positively assessed by the students in the second round. As a result of the new system, the transparency of the game mechanics was perceived to be clearer and was therefore evaluated as better by the students. This even led to a better satisfaction result after the first round. Still, many students complained about the workload, which is why we will reduce the number of challenges and ad hoc tasks to three. The workload for the teaching staff was considerably reduced due to the automatic documentation of the points and the automatic calculation of the leaderboards. With the integration of the *GamEducation* project into the master's level lecture on 'cooperation in e-business', we furthermore changed the examination type from a written to an oral exam. This was part of a reorganisation of our whole master's module, which is why a comparison of the given grades between the basic lecture and the new approach was not significant. Table 11.1 provides an overview of all conducted evaluations; however, not all of the overall 31 questions from the surveys are shown. The qualitative interviews are summarised and, as with the survey questions, grouped into the four main evaluation categories: (a) learning efficiency, (b) workload, (c) motivation and fun and (d) participation and game mechanics.

Table 11.1 Conducted evaluations

First year											

(1) Pre-test with 25 participants before the course

Open to new teaching methods		Expected learning efficiency				Expected fun					
Yes	No	Better		Worse		More		Less			
92 %	8 %	64 %		36 %		88 %		12 %			

(2) Main-test after the course

(a) Learning efficiency			(b) Workload			(c) Motivation and fun			(d) Participation and game mechanics		
A = strongly agree and agree; N = neutral; D = disagree and strongly disagree											
A	N	D	A	N	D	A	N	D	A	N	D

(2.1) Survey with 22 participants

(i) The new approach motivated me to participate more than usual			(i) The workload of the challenges was reasonable			(i) I was satisfied overall with the new teaching approach			(i) I experienced the active participation as promoting the competition		
14	6	2	6	0	16	15	5	2	15	3	4
(ii) The application of the lecture material in the challenges helped me to better understand the overall content of the lecture			(ii) The workload of the ad hoc tasks was reasonable			(ii) I participated actively because I had fun gaining points			(ii) I participated actively because I wanted to have a good position in the ranking		
15	5	2	11	0	11	13	6	3	8	0	7
(iii) I estimate my personal learning efficiency as good			(iii) The workload of the lecture was reasonable			(iii) I was motivated to actively participate in the lecture			(iii) I participated actively because I wanted my group to get a good ranking		
14	6	2	6	0	16	14	3	5	16	3	3

(2.2) Qualitative interviews with 10 participants (Summary)

The active participation, the challenges and the ad hoc tasks led to a better understanding of the lecture material			The workload was generally perceived as too much. Additional insights into the group size and the system used were given			The GamEducation approach motivated students to participate more and it was fun			The active participation of the students was mentioned as positive, but the composition of the points should be explained better		

Second year											

Qualitative interviews with 20 participants (Summary)

The experienced learning efficiency was good. Higher satisfaction thanks to the system			The workload was generally perceived as too much			The lecture motivated students to participate more and the level of fun was evaluated as high			The new system enabled a better understanding of the points system		

11.4   Conclusion and Discussion

With our approach of bringing game mechanics to university teaching we developed the construct *GamEducation*. In order to improve learning efficiency by motivating students to actively participate, *GamEducation* follows the concept of gamification. This led us to hypothesise that university teaching could be improved. *GamEducation* was successfully conducted twice over two years in a master's level course at the University of Technology in Braunschweig. Evaluations showed that *GamEducation* can improve teaching efficiency, motivation and fun, and can lead to more intense participation and a better understanding of the lecture material. However, the implementation of *GamEducation* also comes with negative side effects, such as highly increased workload for both the students and the teaching staff. *GamEducation* means more participation for the students and therefore more mentoring and assistance work for the teaching staff. With the help of the *GamEducation* system, the teaching workload can be reduced but still remains higher than the workload of a traditional frontal lecture.

One condition for gaining funding from the *teach4TU* project was the possibility to transfer the construct to other lectures and seminars. An important aspect was the independence from the teaching material, meaning that the concept of *GamEducation* could be implemented in different fields of study. Therefore, we defined a list of requirements that a lecture or seminar should fulfil in order to implement the concept of *GamEducation*. The first requirement is to have a background story (1) or main task, which is part of the challenges the groups have to work on. According to this the lecture material (2) should be shortened or appropriate to allow time for the groups to present and discuss their challenges. The lecture material and the background story should provide the opportunity to create challenges (3). The number of students (4) should be sufficient for creating more than two groups. In order to handle the teaching workload a system (5) should be used that is able to document all students' contributions and display the leaderboards.

In summary, *GamEducation* is a new approach which provides benefits to many aspects of university teaching. However, it requires specific adjustments to a lecture or seminar and it creates a higher workload for both students and teaching staff.

References

Bligh, D. A. (1998). *What's the use of lectures?* Exeter: Intellect Books.
Coates, H., James, R., & Baldwin, G. (2005). A critical examination of the effects of learning management systems on university teaching and learning. *Tertiary Education and Management, 11*(1), 19–36.
Costikyan, G. (2006). I have no words and I must design: Toward a critical vocabulary for games. In K. Salen & E. Zimmerman (Eds.), *The game design reader: A rules of play anthology*. Cambridge: MIT Press.

Crawford, C. (2004). *Chris Crawford on interactive storytelling*. Berkeley: New Riders.

Dansky, J. L. (1980). Cognitive consequences of sociodrama play and exploration training for economically disadvantaged preschollers. *Journal of Child Psychology and Psychiatry, 21*(1), 47–58.

Deterding, S., Khaled, R., Nacke, L. E., & Dixon, D. (2011). *Gamification: Toward a definition*. Paper presented at the CHI 2011 Workshop Gamification. VanCouver, Canada.

Dickey, M. (2007). Game design and learning: A conjectural analysis of how massively multiple online role-playing games (MMORPGs) foster intrinsic motivation. *Educational Technology Research and Development, 55*(3), 253–273.

Formanek, R. (1991). Why they collect: Collectors reveal their motivations. *Journal of Social Behavior & Personality, 6*(6), 275–286.

Füller, J., Möslein, K. M., Huttner, K., & Haller, J. B. A. (2010). Evaluation games: How to make the crowd your jury. K. P. Fähnrich & B. Franyzyk (Eds.), *Lecture Notes Informatics Proceedings, P-175* (pp. 955–960).

Fullerton, T., Swain, C., & Hoffman, S. (2004). *Game design workshop: Designing, prototyping, and playtesting games*. San Francisco: CMP Books.

Greenblatt, C. S., & Duke, R. D. (1981). *Principles and Practices of Gaming – Simulation*. London: Sage.

Hacker, S., & Ahn, L. (2009). Matchin: Elicting user preferences with online game. In *Proceedings of the 27th International Conference on Human Factors in Computing Systems* (pp. 1207–1216). Boston, MA.

Jackson, G. T., & McNamara, D. S. (2013). Motivation and performance in a game-based intelligent tutoring system. *Journal of Educational Psychology, 105*(4), 1036–1049.

Järvinen, A. (2008). *Games without frontiers: Theories and methods for game studies and design*. Tampere: Tampere University Press.

Jin, S. A. (2009). Avatars mirroring the actual self versus projecting the ideal self: The effects of self-priming on interactivity and immersion in an exergame. *Wii Fit, CyberPsychology & Behavior, 12*(6), 761–765.

Kim, A. J. (2009). Putting the fun in functional. Applying Game Mechanics to Social Media presented at Startup2Startup, Palo Alto, California.

Knautz, K., & Soubusta, S. (2013). *Aufbruch nach Zyren: Game-based Learning in der Hochschullehre*. Hildesheim: Universitätsbibliothek Hildesheim.

Kruse, V., Plicht, C., Spannagel, J., Wehrle, M., & Spannagel, C. (2014). Creatures of the Night: Konzeption und Evaluation einer Gamification-Plattform im Rahmen einer Mathematikvorlesung. In C. Rensing & S. Trahasch (Hrsg.), *Proceedings der Pre-Conference Workshops der 12. e-Learning Fachtagung Informatik DeLFI 2014* (S. 246–253). Aachen: CEUR.

Laurillard, D. (2002). *Rethinking university teaching: A conversational framework for the effective use of learning technologies*. New York: RoutledgeFalmer.

Lee, J. J., & Hammer, J. (2011). Gamification in education: What, how, why bother? *Academic Exchange Quarterly, 15*(2), 1–5.

Mallon, B., & Webb, B. (2000). Structure, causality, visibility and interaction: Propositions for evaluating engagement in narrative multimedia. *International Journal of Human-Computer Studies, 53*(2), 269–287.

McGonigal, J. (2011). *Reality is broken. Why games make us better and how they can change the world*. New York: Pinguin Press.

Reeves, B., & Read, J. L. (2009). *Total engagement: Using games and virtual words to change the way people work and business complete*. New York: McGraw-Hill Professional.

Russ, S. W. (1996). Development of creative processes in children. M Runco (Ed.), *Creativity from childhood through adulthood: The development issues: New directions for child and adolescent development* (pp. 31–42), San Francisco: Jossey Bass.

Salen, K., & Zimmerman, E. (2004). *Rules of play: Game design fundamentals*. Cambridge, MA: MIT Press.

Selwyn, N. (2007). The use of computer technology in university teaching and learning: A critical perspective. *Journal of Computer Assisted learning, 23*(2), 83–94.

Sicart, M. (2008). Defining game mechanics. *The International Journal of Computer Game Research, 8*(2), 1–14.

Tolmie, A., & Boyle, J. (2000). Factors influencing the success of computer mediated communication (CMC) environments in university teaching: A review and case study. *Computers & Education, 34*(2), 119–140.

Webster, J., & Martocchio, J. J. (1992). Microcomputer playfulness: Development of a measure with workplace implications. *MIS Quarterly, 16*(2), 201–226.

Witt, M. (2013). *Application of game mechanics to innovation management: Theoretical foundations and empirical studies.* Ph.D thesis, Technical University of Braunschweig. Available from: http://www.digibib.tu-bs.de/?docid=00050688. Accessed December 18, 2014.

Printed in the United States
By Bookmasters